Confrontation and Other Essays

Rabbi Joseph B. Soloveitchik

Confrontation and Other Essays

Maggid Books

Confrontation and Other Essays

First Maggid Edition, 2015

Maggid Books
An imprint of Koren Publishers Jerusalem Ltd.
POB 8531, New Milford, CT 06776-8531, USA
& POB 4044, Jerusalem 91040, Israel
www.korenpub.com

© Haym Soloveitchik 2015

Cover Photo: Yeshiva University
Spine photo: courtesy of the family of Rabbi Irwin Albert *z"l*

All rights reserved. No part of this publication may be reproduced, stored in a retrieval system or transmitted in any form or by any means, electronic, mechanical, photocopying or otherwise, without the prior permission of the publisher, except in the case of brief quotations embedded in critical articles or reviews.

ISBN 978-1-59264-411-7, *hardcover*

A CIP catalogue record for this title is available from the British Library

Printed and bound in the United States

Contents

The Community 1

Majesty and Humility 25

Catharsis 41

Redemption, Prayer, Talmud Torah 63

Confrontation 85

Publication Information 121

The Community

*Dedicated to the Memory of
The Rebbitzen of Talne, Rebecca Twersky,
A Woman of Valor – 1 Tevet, 5736*

The very instant we pronounce the word "community" we recall, by sheer association, the ancient controversy between collectivism and individualism. Willy nilly the old problem of who and what comes first (metaphysically, not chronologically) arises. Is the individual an independent free entity, who gives up basic aspects of his sovereignty in order to live within a communal framework; or is the reverse true: the individual is born into the community which, in turn, invests him with certain rights? This perennial controversy is still unresolved.

Today the controversy transcends the limits of theoretical debate. People try to resolve it, not by propounding theories or by participating in philosophical symposia in the halls of academia, but by resorting to violence and bloodshed in the

---

This essay was delivered at the 78th annual meeting of the Conference of Jewish Communal Service in Boston, May 31, 1976.

jungles of Asia and Africa. The political confrontation between the West and the East is, *ipso facto*, a philosophical encounter between one-sided collectivism and one-sided individualism.

Let us ask a simple question: what does Judaism say about this conflict?

And let us give a simple answer: Judaism rejects both alternatives; neither theory, *per se*, is true. Both experiences, that of aloneness, as well as that of togetherness, are inseparable basic elements of the I-awareness.

The Bible tells us that God created a single individual, a lonely being:

> וייצר ה׳ אלקים את האדם עפר מן האדמה ויפח באפיו נשמת חיים ויהי האדם לנפש חיה.

> Then the Lord God formed man of the dust of the ground and breathed into his nostrils a breath of life and the man became a living soul.[1]

The Bible also tells us that the Almighty, having created Adam, said:

> לא טוב היות האדם לבדו אעשה לו עזר כנגדו.

> It is not good that the man should be alone; I will make a helpmeet for him.[2]

God created Eve and brought her to Adam.

---

1. Genesis 2:7.
2. Genesis 2:18.

The Community

ויבן ה׳ אלקים את הצלע אשר לקח מן האדם לאשה ויבאה אל האדם.

And the rib which the Lord God had taken from man made He a woman and brought her unto the man.[3]

Who comes first – the community, the pair, or man (or woman) alone? Who takes precedence – Adam and Eve in the utter loneliness which both of them experienced at the hour of creation, or Adam and Eve as a couple, after they had been brought together to become united in marriage?

As we have indicated before, both the community-related and the lonely individual, be he man, be she woman, were created by God. Hence, it would be absurd to equate the Biblical doctrine with either philosophical alternative. The answer to the problem is rather a dialectical one, namely, man is both. He is a single, lonely being, not belonging to any structured collectivity. He is also a thou-related being, who co-exists in companionship with somebody else.

In fact, the greatness of man manifests itself in his inner contradiction, in his dialectical nature, in his being single and unrelated to anyone, as well as in his being thou-related and belonging to a community structure.

Let us investigate this strange philosophy of man, which seems to embrace two mutually exclusive outlooks.

Permit me, however, to preface the analysis with the following remarks.

---

3. Genesis 2:19.

1. Judaism deals with the problem of individualism versus collectivism, not at a socio-economic, but rather at an existential-metaphysical level. Judaism is not concerned with the problem which intrigued many philosophers of the age of reason – whether or not man is a self-sufficient being, whether a Robinson Crusoe is reality or fantasy. Judaism asks a completely different question. Was the human charisma, the *imago dei*, bestowed upon solitary, lonely man or upon man within a social frame of reference? In retreat or in togetherness – where does man find his true self?

2. The community in Judaism is not a functional-utilitarian, but an ontological one. The community is not just an assembly of people who work together for their mutual benefit, but a metaphysical entity, an individuality; I might say, a living whole. In particular, Judaism has stressed the wholeness and the unity of *Knesset Israel*, the Jewish community. The latter is not a conglomerate. It is an autonomous entity, endowed with a life of its own. We, for instance, lay claim to *Eretz Israel*. God granted the land to us as a gift. To whom did He pledge the land? Neither to an individual, nor to a partnership consisting of millions of people. He gave it to the *Knesset Israel*, to the community as an independent unity, as a distinct juridic metaphysical person. He did not promise the land to me, to you, to them; nor did He promise the land to all of us together. Abraham did not receive the land as an individual, but as the father of a future nation. The owner of the Promised Land is the *Knesset Israel*, which is a community persona. However strange such a concept may appear to the empirical sociologist, it is not at all a strange experience for the Halachist and the mystic, to whom *Knesset Israel* is a living, loving, and suffering mother.

The Community

3. The personalistic unity and reality of a community, such as *Knesset Israel*, is due to the philosophy of existential complementarity of the individuals belonging to the *Knesset Israel*.[4] The individuals belonging to the community complement one another existentially. Each individual possesses something unique, rare, which is unknown to others; each individual has a unique message to communicate, a special color to add to the communal spectrum. Hence, when lonely man joins the community, he adds a new dimension to the community awareness. He contributes something which no one else could have contributed. He enriches the community existentially; he is irreplaceable. Judaism has always looked upon the individual as if he were a little world (microcosm);[5] with the death of the individual, this little world comes to an end. A vacuum which other individuals cannot fill is left. The saying: כל המקיים נפש אחת, כאלו קיים עולם מלא, "Whoever saves one life, it is as if had saved the entire world,"[6] should be understood in this way. The sensitive Halachic rules pertaining to mourning (*avelut*) are rooted in the Halacha's perception of the tragic singleness of man, in the awareness that man as a natural being exists once in an eternity. Because of that singleness, individuals get together, complement each other, and attain ontological wholeness.

---

4. The Halachic principle of אין צבור מתים, "A congregation does not die" (*Temurah* 15b), is rooted in the concept we have indicated, namely, that the existence of the community as a metaphysical unity surpasses the physical existence of its individual members. Vide also Nahmanides, Genesis 24:1 s.v. *bakol*.
5. This idea is basic in the philosophy of Ibn Gabirol and attains its classic formulation in Maimonides' *Guide*, I, 72.
6. Mishnah *Sanhedrin* 4:5.

These two traits of the community (individuality and complementarity), we find in the Biblical portrayal of the marriage-community. The latter consists of two unique personalities. The male and the female represent two different existential experiences; man and woman differ, not only as natural beings, but as metaphysical personae as well. Man is man in all his thoughts and feelings, while the same is true of the woman: she is a woman in her whole existential experience. When both join in matrimony, a community of two "incommensurate" beings is formed. Woman and man complement each other existentially: together they form, not a partnership, but an individuality, a persona. The marriage-community is like the general community; its strength lies, not in that which is common to the participants, but in their singularity and singleness.

3

Now let us proceed with the analysis of the individual vis-à-vis the community.

What does it mean to be alone? It signifies, not physical distance, but ontological-existential remoteness, or ontological-existential alienation of the I from the thou, regardless of how close the thou and the I may be.

Two people love one another. The young handsome husband and the young lovely wife are dedicated unqualifiedly to each other. They share joy and grief together. Suddenly, God forbid, disaster strikes. One of the two loving mates takes sick; the prognosis is discouraging. What happens in such a situation?

At the very outset the loving mate who enjoys good health finds himself in a state of shock. He or she simply cannot imagine a life without the participation of the other person in all occasions of joy and anxiety. He or she is exposed to black, cruel despair; temporarily, he or she lives in a state of complete mental dislocation, bordering on insanity. Life becomes, for him or for her, an absurdity, a nauseating affair, ugly and monstrous. However, with the passage of time and the gradual assimilation of the cruel prognosis into his or her mind, the ruthless process of alienation sets in. The sick person and the loving mate begin to drift, to move away from each other, and the process of estrangement reaches frightening proportions. Love turns into indifference; the latter, into hostility. The once-loving mate begins to resent the mere fact that he, or she, must stay in one room with the sick person. He or she is angry at the sick person because the latter is still alive. The ontological remoteness between the once-loving mates reaches fantastic proportions.[7]

4

I have tried to portray ontological alienation in radical, harsh terms, depicting a grisly and awesome situation in which love is replaced by fear, hysterical confusion and brutish cruelty. However, ontological remoteness and alienation can be observed even under normal circumstances. I dare say that, in everyday life, alienation or existential detachment is proportionate to the intensity and depth of emotional attachment. The more intense the sense of dedication and love, the greater the disappointment or estrangement. There is, in every love-experience, a streak of alienation; the greater the love-experience, the stronger the streak of alienation. A young mother, drunk with love

---

7. Leo Tolstoy, in his classic story *The Death of Ivan Ilich*, portrays such a tragic spectacle of alienation and loneliness.

for her pink-cheeked baby and her young husband, is awakened, at two in the morning, by the darling girl. The tired, exhausted mother tries to quiet the baby and put her back to sleep. Her husband does not stir; she wonders: Is he asleep or awake? The young mother, who carries the load alone, whose patience is at breaking point, whispers bitterly: What do you both want of me? Why is there no sympathy for me? For a short while she rejects both daughter and husband. For a few seconds ontological remoteness separates them. Whether the young mother is right or wrong in her brief rebellion against the institution of marriage is irrelevant. What is relevant is that, for a few seconds, she has withdrawn from a together-existence into existential remoteness and solitude. She has become, for an infinitesimal moment, conscious of her loneliness, despite the fact that she is happily married. For a fraction of a second she has identified herself with the man or woman created alone that mysterious Friday.

Of course, psychology is rich in nomenclature, and has many terms to describe such behavior. Judaism, however, is concerned, not with behavioral patterns, but with the existential experience. Existentially, man realizes quite often that he is lonely, and that all talk about being together is just an illusion.

5

Why was it necessary to create lonely man? Why was social man not created at the very outset?

1. The originality and creativity in man are rooted in his loneliness-experience, not in his social awareness. The singleness of man is responsible for his singularity;

the latter, for his creativity. Social man is superficial: he imitates, he emulates. Lonely man is profound: he creates, he is original.

2. Lonely man is free; social man is bound by many rules and ordinances. God willed man to be free. Man is required, from time to time, to defy the world, to replace the old and obsolete with the new and relevant. Only lonely man is capable of casting off the harness of bondage to society. Who was Abraham? Who was Elijah? Who were the prophets? People who dared rebuke society in order to destroy the *status quo* and replace it with a new social order. The story of Judaism is not only that of the community but also of man alone, confronted by the many. "What doest thou here Elijah?"

מה לך פה אליהו?
ויאמר קנא קנאתי לה׳ אלקי צבקות כי עזבו בריתך בני ישראל את מזבחתיך הרסו ואת נביאיך הרגו בחרב; ואותר אני לבדי ויבקשו את נפשי לקחתה.

I have been very zealous for the Lord, the God of hosts; for the children of Israel have forsaken Thy covenant, cast down Thine altars and slain Thy prophets; and I, even I only, am left and they seek my life ...[8]

In other words: "I am remote from my people; there is complete alienation. I am a lonely individual, I defy the community, I rebel against the nation." The *levado*-awareness is the root of heroic defiance. Heroism is the central category in practical

---

8. 1 Kings 19:9–10.

Judaism. The Torah wanted the Jew to live heroically, to rebuke, reproach, condemn, whenever society is wrong and unfair. The *levado* gives the Jew the heroic arrogance which makes it possible for him to be different. Did not the Jew display heroic arrogance by defying the world throughout the millennia? Does not tiny Israel exhibit heroic arrogance in rejecting the U.N.? Don't we American Jews experience a sense of heroic loneliness and alienation from the general society, whenever the problem of Israel comes up in a conversation, and we recognize the incommensurability of our viewpoint with that of the international political community? Lonely man is a courageous man; he is a protester; he fears nobody; whereas social man is a compromiser, a peacemaker, and at times a coward. At first man had to be created *levado*, alone; for otherwise he would have lacked the courage or the heroic quality to stand up and to protest, to act like Abraham, who took the ax and shattered the idols which his own father had manufactured.

6

However, man was created a second time. He fell asleep a lonely man and awoke to find Eve standing beside him. God willed man to exist in solitude, to experience aloneness. He also willed man to break out of his loneliness, to move closer to the thou, and to share the existential experience with the thou.

To exist alone is not good – said the Lord God. Man is not only a protester; he is an affirmer too. He is not only an iconoclast, but a builder, as well. If man always felt remote from everybody and everything, then the very purpose of creation could not be achieved. Moses was both the greatest loner, who pitched his tent הרחק מן המחנה – "far outside the camp," and, at the same time, the great leader, father and teacher of the people to whom the whole community clung:

The Community

ויהי ממחרת ... ויעמד העם על משה מן הבקר עד הערב.

And the people stood before Moses from the morning until the evening.[9]

In a word, man, in order to realize himself, must be alone, but, at the same time, he must be a member of a community.

II

I

How is the community formed? The answer is simple: two lonely individuals create a community in the manner that God created the world. What was God's instrument of creation? The word. The word is also the instrument with which man creates his own community. God, by saying *yehi*, which is identical with an act of recognition of the world, made it possible for a beside-Him existence to emerge, made it possible for finitude to co-exist with infinity, notwithstanding that, as a mathematical equation, finitude + infinity = infinity, or, in other words, that the co-existence of the infinite and the finite is an impossibility. God, in order to make "room" for the finite world, employed *middat hatzimtzum*, the method of self-contraction or self-limitation, *kivyakhol*. He withdrew, and by engaging in a movement of recoil, *kivyakhol*, He precipitated "empty space" for the world. Otherwise the latter could not have come into existence, since it would have been "swallowed" by infinity. Thus, we may suggest the following equation: creation = recognition = withdrawal = an act of sacrifice.

The same is true of man. If lonely man is to rise from existential exclusiveness to existential all-inclusiveness, then the first thing he has to do is to recognize another existence. Of course

---

9. Exodus 33:7; 18:13.

this recognition is, *eo ipso*, a sacrificial act, since the mere admission that a thou exists in addition to the I, is tantamount to *tzimtzum*, self-limitation and self-contraction. A community is established the very moment I recognize the thou and extend greetings to the thou. One individual extends the *shalom* greeting to another individual; and in so doing he creates a community. The Halacha has attached great significance to casual greetings exchanged between two individuals. Rabbi Helbo said: "If his friend greets him and he does not return the greeting he is called a robber, for it is said, 'It is ye that have eaten up the vineyard, the spoil of the poor is in your houses.'"[10] What message does *Shalom* convey, if not encouragement and solace to the lonely and distressed? The Halacha commands us to return greetings, and in some cases to extend them, even during the recital of *Shema*.[11] To recognize somebody by greeting him or responding to a greeting does not contradict the performance of *kabbalat ol malchut Shamayim* (acceptance of the yoke of Heaven). Halacha says to man: Don't let your neighbor drift along the lanes of loneliness; don't permit him to become remote and alienated from you, even when you are busy reciting *Shema*. If God willed a world to rise from nihility in order to bestow His love upon this world, then lonely man should affirm the existence of somebody else in order to have the opportunity of giving love. Again the same equation prevails: recognition *means* sacrificial action; the individual withdraws in order to make room for the thou.

2

Quite often a man finds himself in a crowd among strangers. He feels lonely. No one knows him, no one cares for him, no

---

10. *Brakhot* 6a; verse cited from Isaiah 3:14.
11. Mishnah *Brakhot* 2:1.

one is concerned with him. It is again an existential experience. He begins to doubt his ontological worth. This leads to alienation from the crowd surrounding him. Suddenly someone taps him on the shoulder and says: "Aren't you Mr. So-and-So? I have heard so much about you." In a fraction of a second his awareness changes. An alien being turns into a fellow member of an existential community (the crowd). What brought about the change? The recognition by somebody, the word!

To recognize a person is not just to identify him physically. It is more than that: it is an act of identifying him existentially, as a person who has a job to do, that only he can do properly. To recognize a person means to affirm that he is irreplaceable. To hurt a person means to tell him that he is expendable, that there is no need for him.

The Halacha equated the act of publicly embarrassing a person with murder.[12] Why? Because humiliation is tantamount to destroying an existential community and driving the individual into solitude. It is not enough for the charitable person to extend help to the needy. He must do more than that: he must try to restore to the dependent person a sense of dignity and worth. That is why Jews have developed special sensitivity regarding orphans and widows, since these persons are extremely sensitive and lose their self-confidence at the slightest provocation. The Bible warned us against afflicting an orphan or a widow.

What kind of an affliction does the Bible prohibit? Murder, mutilation, causing of severe pain, destruction of property, etc.? Not only these, but lesser evils, as well. Whatever affects the peace of mind of the widow or the orphan is considered affliction. A word, a gesture, a facial expression by which the

---

12. *Baba Metzia* 58b: כל המלבין פני חבירו ברבים כאילו שופך דמים.

widow or the orphan feels hurt; in short, whatever causes an accelerated heartbeat — that comes under affliction.

וכשנאחזו רבן שמעון ורבי ישמעאל וגזרו עליהן שיהרגו היה רבן שמעון בוכה, ואמר לו רבי ישמעאל: ברבי! בשתי פסיעות אתה נתון בחיקן של צדיקים ואתה בוכה? אמר לו: ... בוכה אני על שאנו נהרגין כשופכי דמים וכמחללי שבתות. אמר לו: שמא בסעודה היית יושב או ישן היית, ובאתה אשה לשאול על נדתה ועל טומאתה ועל טהרתה ואמר לה השמש שהיית ישן, והתורה אמרה אם ענה תענה אותו, ומה כתיב אחריו - ... והרגתי אתכם בחרב.

> When R. Shimon b. Gamaliel and R. Ishmael appeared [before the Romans], and were condemned to death, R. Shimon wept, and R. Ishmael said: "Sir, you are but two steps from the bosom of the righteous, and yet you weep?" He answered: "... I weep because we are being executed as if we were murderers ..." To which [R. Ishmael] answered: "Perhaps you were at the table or asleep, and a woman came to inquire about her ritual purity, and the attendant told her: 'He is asleep'; for the Torah said: 'If you torment them [the widow and orphan] ...,' and continued: 'Then I shall kill you by the sword.'"[13]

What was wrong in R. Shimon's conduct? He had come home exhausted after a full day's work, and lay down for a short rest. It had been a busy day: the entire load of communal responsibilities pressed heavily on his frail shoulders. Cruel Rome continued its ruthless policy of religious persecution and economic

---

13. Tractate *Semahot* 8:8; verse cited from Exodus 22:22–23; variant in *Mekhilta of R. Ishmael* on Exodus (*Mishpatim, Masekhta deNezikin*, 18).

The Community

ruin of the people. R. Shimon b. Gamaliel had to perform an almost impossible task, to negotiate with, as well as to defy the conquerors; to communicate with his Jewish brethren, telling them not to despair, and at the same time to ready them for rebellion and the supreme sacrifice.

While he was dozing, a woman entered with an inquiry: is she ritually pure or impure? The attendant, knowing how fatigued R. Shimon was, advised her to wait until he awoke; he did not wish to disturb R. Shimon. How, then, the question arises, did R. Shimon afflict the woman? The woman was a poor widow, and extremely sensitive. While waiting for R. Shimon, the thought went through her head: had my rich neighbor come with a similar question, the attendant would have acted differently: he would have aroused R. Shimon. Because of my poverty and loneliness, she thought, he didn't mind making me wait; she sighed, and brushed away a tear. So R. Shimon did afflict a widow, and thus violated a Biblical prohibition. Her tear was responsible for the tragic death of R. Shimon: אחד עוני מרובה ואחד עוני מועט, "A great affliction and a small affliction are all the same."[14] The degree of hurt is irrelevant; causing transient humiliation and causing severe physical pain are both subsumed under affliction.

III

I

Once I have recognized the thou and invited him to join the community, I ipso facto assumed responsibility for the thou. Recognition is identical with commitment.

Here again we walk in the ways of our Maker. God created man; God did not abandon him; God showed concern for him. God cared for Adam: God said: It is not good for man

---

14. *Mekhilta* version, *ibid.*

to be alone. He provided him with a mate; He placed him in Paradise, and allowed him to enjoy the fruit of the Garden. Even after man sinned and was exiled from the Garden, the Almighty did not desert him. Of course, He punished him. Yet He was concerned with man even while man was in sin. In a word, God assumed responsibility for whatever and whomever He created:

נותן לחם לכל בשר כי לעולם חסדו.

> He gives bread to all flesh for His loving-kindness is everlasting.[15]

As we have said above, the same relationship should prevail between me and the thou whom I have recognized, and with whom I have formed a community. I assume responsibility for each member of the community to whom I have granted recognition and whom I have found worthy of being my companion. In other words, the I is responsible for the physical and mental welfare of the thou.

2

When the I becomes aware of his being responsible for the well-being of the thou, whom he has helped bring into existence, a new community emerges: the community of prayer. What does this mean? It means a community of common pain, of common suffering. The Halacha has taught the individual to include his fellow man in his prayer. The individual must not limit himself to his own needs, no matter how pressing those needs are and how distinguished he is. Halacha has formulated prayer in the plural. There is hardly a prayer which avails itself

---

15. Psalm 136:25. Vide Maimonides' *Guide* III, 54.

of the grammatical singular. Even private prayers, such as those offered on the occasion of sickness, death, or other crises, are recited in the plural.

המקום ינחם אתכם בתוך שאר אבלי ציון וירושלים.

May the Almighty comfort thee among all mourners of Zion and Jerusalem.

שתשלח רפואה שלמה מן השמים... בתוך שאר חולי ישראל.

I beseech Thee to cure this individual as well as other sick people and restore them to full health.[16]

Whatever the needs, the prayer must not be confined to an individual. Moses prayed for the community forty days in succession, and God tolerated his intercession on behalf of the community. Indeed, He granted atonement to the people.

---

16. *Shabbat* 12a-b:

ת״ר הנכנס לבקר את החולה אומר... רבי יהודה אומר: המקום ירחם עליך ועל חולי ישראל; רבי יוסי אומר: המקום ירחם עליך בתוך חולי ישראל (רש״י: שמתוך שכוללן עם האחרים תפילתו נשמעת בזכותן של רבים).

> The Rabbis taught: When one visits the sick ... one says, according to R. Judah: "May God have mercy on you *and* other sick people of Israel"; according to R. Jose: "May God have mercy on you *among* other sick people of Israel." (Rashi: Through inclusion of the others, his prayer is heard, for the sake of the many.)

Brakhot 29b-30a:

אמר אביי: לעולם לישתף אינש נפשיה בהדי צבורא (רש״י: אל יתפלל תפלה קצרה בלשון יחיד אלא בלשון רבים שמתוך כך תפלתו נשמעת).

> Abbaye said: One should always include oneself together with the community. (Rashi: Let him not pray ... in the singular but in the plural; for through this, his prayer is heard.)

> ואתנפל לפני ה' כראשונה ארבעים יום וארבעים לילה. לחם לא אכלתי ומים לא שתיתי על כל חטאתכם.

And I fell before the Lord as before forty days and forty nights; I did not eat bread or drink water, for all your sins.[17]

On another occasion, however, when Moses tried to pray to the Almighty, God stopped him in the middle. He did not permit him to continue praying; neither did He grant his wish. Moses prayed for himself; the Almighty rejected the prayer.

> ואתחנן אל ה' בעת ההיא לאמר... אעברה נא ואראה את הארץ הטובה אשר בעבר הירדן ההר הטוב הזה והלבנון. ויתעבר ה' בי למענכם ולא שמע אלי ויאמר ה' אלי רב לך אל תוסף דבר אלי עוד בדבר הזה.

And I besought the Lord at that time saying … "O Lord God … let me go over and see the good land that is beyond the Jordan, that goodly hill country and Lebanon." But the Lord was wroth with me … and harkened not unto me, and the Lord said unto me: "Let it suffice; speak no more unto Me of this matter."[18]

When Moses' prayer was recited in the plural, all the gates of prayer were open and the Lord allowed him to intercede many, many days for the people. When Moses changed his prayer to the singular, the gates of prayer and loving-kindness were slammed in his face.

The Midrash states that, had the community joined Moses in his prayer, God would have granted the request. He would

---

17. Deuteronomy 9:18.
18. Deuteronomy 3:23–26.

not have rejected the prayer of the many.[19] Unfortunately, the community did not understand the secret of prayer-by-the-many. As a consequence of their ignorance, Moses died in the desert.

The individual prayer usually revolves about physical pain, mental anguish, or suffering which man cannot bear anymore. At the level of individual prayer, prayer does not represent the singularly human need. Even a mute creature in the field reacts to physical pain with a shriek or outcry. Such a reaction was, to be sure, equated with prayer:

שומע תפלה עדיך כל בשר יבאו.

Hearer of prayer, unto You all flesh must come.[20]

However, prayer in the plural is a unique human performance. Why do I use the plural form when I pray? Because I am aware, not only of my pain, but of the pain of the many, because I share in the suffering of the many. Again, it is not psychological; it is rather existential awareness of pain. The I suffers the pain of millions. The I is sensitive to the pain of all people. Said Yehuda Halevi:

---

19. *Sifre* (Deuteronomy 3:24):

בשעה שסרחו במעשה העגל ... עמדתי והתפללתי עליהם ושמעת תפילתי וסלחת לעוונם, הייתי סבור שאני עמהם בתפלה והם לא התפללו עלי. והלא דברים קל וחומר: אם תפלת יחיד על הרבים כך נשמעת, תפלת הרבים על היחיד על אחת כמה וכמה?

When they made the calf ... I stood up and prayed for them and You heard my prayer and forgave their sin; I thought that I was with them in prayer, but they did not pray for me. It should be *à forteriori*: if the prayer of an individual for the many was heard, the prayer of the many for the individual so much more?

20. Psalm 65:3.

ישראל באומות כלב באברים ... שהלב בזכוך הרגשתו ... הוא מרגיש בדבר המועט שיפגעהו.

> The people of Israel among the nations is like the heart in the body... the heart ... is sensitive to the slightest trauma.[21]

Knesset Israel is a prayerful community, in which every individual experiences, not only his pain, but also that of countless others. I still remember the distress we young boys experienced when we heard of a pogrom in some Jewish town thousands of miles away. Our anguish was due not to fear, but to sympathy and compassion. We felt the pain of the nation as a whole. Our glorious charity-tradition, through the ages, is the result of our having been a prayerful, compassionate community.

3

The prayer community, it is self-evident, must at the same time be a charity-community, as well. It is not enough to feel the pain of many, nor is it sufficient to pray for the many, if this does not lead to charitable action. Hence, *Knesset Israel* is not only a prayerful community but a charitable community, too. We give, we pray for all because we are sensitive to pain; we try to help the many. We Jews have developed a singular sensitivity to pain which is characteristic of the Jew. The term for it – רחמנות, *rahmanut* – is a Hebrew word, most commonly used as a Yiddish colloquialism derived from the Hebrew, רחם, רחמן.
    What is the semantics of רחמן, *rahman*, in contrast with that of מרחם, *merahem*? *Merahem* denotes an activity; it tells us one thing, namely, that a particular person acts with mercy; the

---

21. Kuzari II:36–41.

word does not reveal to us what motivates those acts. *Rahman*, in contradistinction with *merahem*, tells us, not only that a person acts with kindness, but that he is himself, by his very nature, kind. The *rahman* commiserates, as if he had no choice in the matter; he is kind because his kindness is compulsive.[22] *Rahmanut* describes kindness as a trait of personality. *Rahmanut*, then, signifies utter sensitivity to pain, and describes beautifully the specific, unique relationship of a Jew to suffering.

4

The prayerful-charity community rises to a higher sense of communion in the teaching community, where teacher and disciple are fully united. The teaching community is centered around an adult, the teacher, and a bunch of young vivacious children, with whom he communicates and communes. He is as young as they are; and they are as old as he is. יש לנו אב זקן וילד זקונים קטן, "We have an old father and a young child,"[23] the brothers told Joseph in Egypt.

The central figure in Jewish history has been not the king, nor the field marshal, nor the political leader, but the very old teacher surrounded by very young children.

> והיה כי יאמרו אליכם בניכם מה העבודה הזאת לכם... והגדת לבנך... ושננתם לבניך.
>
> And when your children say to you, "What is this?" ... you shall tell your children ... and repeat to your children.[24]

---

22. Cf. the comment in the Vilna Gaon's Prayer Book, סדור אשי ישראל, p. 442, citing Rashi *Baba Metzia* 33a, ד"ה רובץ ולא רבצן.
23. Genesis 44:20.
24. Exodus 12:26; 13:8; Deuteronomy 6:7.

Rabbi Joseph B. Soloveitchik

What does the teacher do? He tells a story. What is the nature of the story that has been told and retold hundreds of times through the generations? We tell the children the story of laws which form the foundation of Jewish morality; we tell them the story of honesty and sincerity, love and sympathy; this story is meant to teach the child not to steal, not to lie, not to be vindictive. We also try to tell the child the story of statutes whose meaning we do not fully grasp. We tell him the story of *hukkim*, laws whose rationale is beyond our grasp, of man's surrender to his Maker, the story of the suspension of human judgment in deference to a higher will.

We also tell the child the story of people who met God and joined Him in a covenant, who engaged the Almighty in a dialogue; we tell the child the story of our past; we help the child develop a historical memory; we train the child not to forget past events. We tell the child the story of our confrontation with God in the desert; we urge the child not to forget our liberation from bondage and our encounter with Amalek, the destructive Satan. We teach the child to be loyal to those memories, to a land, to a sanctuary, etc.

We not only tell stories describing events; we tell stories precipitating the re-experiences of events which transpired millennia ago. To tell a story is to relive the event. We still sit on the floor and mourn the destruction of the sanctuary, an event which took place 1,900 years ago. We still celebrate the Exodus, an event which lies at the dawn of our history. Our stories are concerned, not only with the past, but with the future, as well. We tell our children the story of patient waiting for the great realization of the promise, no matter how slow the realization is in coming.

In short, it is an exciting story that we tell them. It is the story of a teaching community which cuts across the ages,

The Community

encompassing people who lived millennia ago, who made their contribution to the *Knesset Israel*, and have left the stage. We also tell them the story of people who, at some point in the distant future, will enter the historical stage. Our story unites countless generations; present, past, and future merge into one great experience.

Contrary to the popular medieval adage,[25] our story tells of a glorious past that is still real, because it has not vanished, a future which is already here, and a creative present replete with opportunity and challenge. It is a privilege and a pleasure to belong to such a prayerful, charitable, teaching community, which feels the breath of eternity.

---

25. עבר אין, ועתיד עדין, וההווה כהרף עין, ואם כן דאגה מנין?‏ (quoted in E. Ben Yehuda's Dictionary *s.v.* עבר, vol. 9, pp. 4291–2). It has been translated into English as follows:

The past already gone by;
The future not yet nigh;
　The present must fly
　　Like the blink of an eye:
So wonder: worry? why?!

Majesty and Humility

Man is a dialectical being; an inner schism runs through his personality at every level. This schism is not due to man's revolt against his Maker, as Christian theology has preached since the days of Augustine. Unlike this view, according to which it was man who, by his sinful rebellion against his Maker, precipitated the split in human nature, the Judaic view posits that the schism is willed by God as the source of man's greatness and his election as a singular charismatic being. Man is a great and creative being because he is torn by conflict and is always in a state of ontological tenseness and perplexity. The fact that the creative gesture is associated with agony is a result of this contradiction, which pervades the whole personality of man.

Judaic dialectic, unlike the Hegelian, is irreconcilable and hence interminable. Judaism accepted a dialectic consisting only of thesis and antithesis. The third Hegelian stage, that

---

This essay was delivered at Rutgers University, under the aegis of the B'nai Brith Hillel Foundation, April 14, 1973.

of reconciliation, is missing. The conflict is final, almost absolute. Only God knows how to reconcile; we do not. Complete reconciliation is an eschatological vision. To Hegel, man and his history were just abstract ideas; in the world of abstractions, synthesis is conceivable. To Judaism, man has always been and still is a living reality, or may I say, a tragic living reality. In the world of realities, the harmony of opposites is an impossibility.

The Psalmist proclaimed, אני אמרתי בחפזי כל האדם כוזב, "I said in my haste all men are liars."[1] What kind of lie did the Psalmist have in mind when he hurled this serious accusation at man in general? Did he have in mind the lie which the I tells the thou? Did he refer to the everyday social lie? Did he refer to the commercial lie of the dishonest businessman, to the political lie of the faithless ruler, to the judicial lie of the perjurer? In a word, did he speak of the profitable, immoral lie? Does man indeed engage constantly in immoral lying?[2] By no means! The Psalmist is concerned with a different kind of lie – the existential lie that man tells, not others, but himself. Man is indeed a liar, because he is involved in an unresolvable contradiction, in an insoluble dialectic, because he is caught like Abraham's ram in a thicket of antinomies and dichotomies. He swings like a pendulum between two poles: the thesis and the antithesis, the affirmation and the negation, identifying himself either with both of them or with neither. He must lie, but this inevitable lie is rooted in man's uniqueness and is a moral lie. It is the springwell of human creativity. That agony accompanies the

---

1. Psalm 116:11. Vide Rashi and Ibn Ezra.
2. א״ר סימון בשעה שבא הקב״ה לבראת את אדם הראשון, נעשו מלאכי השרת כיתים כיתים, וחבורות חבורות, מהם אומרים: אל יברא, ומהם אומרים: יברא... ואמת אומר: אל יברא, שכולו שקרים...

R. Simon said: "When God came to the creation of Adam, the angels divided into groups; some said: Let him not be created; and some said: Let him be created … Truth said: 'Let him not be created, for he is all lies'" (*Genesis Rabbah* 8).

process of creativity is due to the fact we mentioned above – that it is torn man who is the creator.

2

It is obvious that dialectical man cannot be committed to a uniform, homogeneous morality. If man is dialectical, so is his moral gesture. Judaism has indeed formulated such a dialectical morality.

There are two objectives which moral man pursues. Man is, quite often, a captive of two enchanting visions, summoning him to move in opposite directions. He is attracted by opposing norms, by two sets of values; two stars infinitely distant from each other beckon to him. Man must decide which alternative to take, which route to choose, which star to follow. The clash is staggering. Man, confused, kneels in prayer, petitioning God, who has burdened him with this dialectic, to guide him and to enlighten him. The Halacha is concerned with this dilemma and tries to help man in such critical moments. The Halacha, of course, did not discover the synthesis, since the latter does not exist. It did, however, find a way to enable man to respond to both calls.

The basic dialectic of man and his morality was beautifully captured in two midrashic homilies quoted by Rashi. In his comment to the verse וייצר ה׳ אלקים את האדם עפר מן האדמה, "And God created man dust of the earth,"[3] Rashi says:

> צבר עפרו מכל האדמה מארבע רוחות וכו׳.

> God gathered the dust [from which man was fashioned] from the entire earth – from its four corners.

---

3. Genesis 2:7.

Rabbi Joseph B. Soloveitchik

ד"א: נטל עפרו ממקום שנאמר בו: מזבח אדמה תעשה לי.

> He took the dust [from which man was made] from that spot which was designated by the Almighty, at the very dawn of creation, as the future site of the altar. As it is written: "An altar of earth thou shalt make unto Me."

Man was created of cosmic dust. God gathered the dust, of which man was fashioned, from all parts of the earth, indeed from all the uncharted lanes of creation. Man belongs everywhere. He is no stranger to any part of the universe. The native son of the sleepy little town is, at the same time, a son of parts distant and unknown. In short, man is a cosmic being.

He is cosmic in a threefold manner:

First, man is cosmic through his intellectual involvement. His intellectual curiosity is of cosmic, universal dimensions. He wants to know, not only about the things that are close to him as, for example, the flowering bush in his backyard, but also about things far removed from him, things and events millions of light years away. Human cosmic inquisitiveness borders almost on the arrogant. Man is restless because he has not yet resolved the *mysterium magnum* of the cosmic drama. Remoteness magnifies, rather than diminishes, man's curiosity. The farther the object, the greater and more hypnotic the curiosity. Man asks himself: to whom does the universe belong? The answer was given by the Psalmist: "The earth is the Lord's and the fullness thereof" – לה' הארץ ומלאה.[4] To whom did God entrust this earth and its fullness? To man who studies and comprehends the cosmic drama. Ownership of the stars, the planets, the dark interplanetary or interstellar spaces, is

---

4. Psalms 24:1.

Majesty and Humility

granted by the Almighty only to those who make the effort to understand them, to those who are curious about them. Man owns the world through his intellectual involvement in it. The old Aristotelian and Maimonidean theorem about the unity of the subject-knower and the object of inquiry, gives man the credentials of cosmic citizenship.

Second, man is cosmic through his experiential involvement; man is cosmos-oriented not only intellectually, but emotionally as well. He loves the cosmos. He, in person, wants to be everywhere. Man is questing, not only to know the universe, but also to experience it. Explorer and adventurer, he feels bored by the monotony and the routine of familiar surroundings. He is out to "see the world." Man is not satisfied sending up unmanned vehicles to gather scientific data. He is eager to do it himself. He wishes to move, with the velocity of light, into a world of the unknown. Man wants to experience and to enjoy vastness. This quest, in contrast to the first, is of an aesthetic rather than an intellectual nature. If we ask again: Who owns the stars? the answer is: Whoever loves them.

Third, man is cosmic through his mobility. Man is a mobile being. He can easily detach himself from native surroundings and adapt himself to new environs. His adaptability to new conditions transcends that of the plant and the animal. The verse in Deuteronomy, כי האדם עץ השדה לבא מפניך במצור,[5] contains a rhetorical question: "Is man like the tree of the field?" Is the tree as mobile as man? Certainly not! Man's greatness and distinctiveness find expression in his ceaseless mobility. The tree is inseparable from the soil. Man can, and does, move away from home.

---

5. Deuteronomy 20:19; following Rashi.

In short, cosmic man[6] is mesmerized by the infinite number of opportunities with which his fantasy presents him. He forgets the simple tragic fact that he is finite and mortal, and that to reach out for infinity and eternity is a foolhardy undertaking.

II

I

Let us examine the other interpretation of the verse in Genesis: man was created from the dust of a single spot. Man is committed to one locus. The Creator assigned him a single spot he calls home. Man is not cosmic; he is here-minded. He is a rooted being, not cosmopolitan but provincial, a villager who belongs to the soil that fed him as a child and to the little world into which he was born.

At this juncture we encounter the old Biblical idea of *nahalah*, inheritance or homestead. We recall the solemn words, spoken with trepidation, by Naboth, in response to Ahab's request that he exchange his vineyard for another one: חלילה לי מה׳ מתתי את נחלת אבתי לך, "The Lord forbid me that I should give the inheritance of my fathers unto thee."[7] Man is rooted in his *nahalah*. When torn away he becomes *na vanad*, another Cain, a restless vagabond, a dislocated being. Homelessness, uprootedness is a curse. Man quests for *nahalah*, for the origin. Because of this origin-consciousness, he is curious to know everything about his roots, about the *makor* which sustains his selfhood.

---

6. It is obvious that the term cosmic man should not be taken literally, as referring exclusively to those who have penetrated interplanetary spaces or those who are committed to this objective. The term is much wider in scope and it characterizes man as a quester and searcher for vastness and boundlessness in any area of endeavor, be it the sciences, be it commerce and industry, be it political community or *hedoné*.
7. 1 Kings 21:3.

Yes, man may roam along the charted and uncharted lanes of the universe, he may reach for the skies. Yet the traveler, the adventurer out to conquer infinity, will surely return home. If this homecoming did not occur during his lifetime, because he was too preoccupied with motion and exploration, it will certainly take place posthumously when his body will be brought home, to the quiet, lonely graveyard which had long been expecting him.

What is the meaning of death in the Biblical tradition? Return! What kind of return? Return to whom, to what? Return to the origin, to the source. עד שובך אל האדמה כי ממנה לקחת כי עפר אתה ואל עפר תשוב, "... till thou return unto the ground for out of it wast thou taken: for dust thou art, and unto dust shalt thou return."[8] The Bible also identified dying with return to the ancestors: ואתה תבא אל אבותיך בשלום, "But thou shalt go to thy fathers in peace."[9] Did not Jacob request of Joseph: ושכבתי עם אבותי ונשאתני ממצרים וקברתני בקבורתם, "Carry me out of Egypt and bury me in their [his ancestors'] burying place"?[10] The old man wanted to rest with his ancestors, the originators of the covenant.

The dust of which man was fashioned was not taken from all parts of the universe, according to the Midrash, but from a single spot on a mountain where an altar was many, many years later constructed. As we said before, each man is created from and attached to a single spot, the origin, from which he cannot escape. The home for which man yearns attracts him like a powerful magnet; it brings him back, no matter how far he has traveled. "Home is the sailor, home from the sea, and

---

8. Genesis 3:19.
9. *Ibid.*, 15:15.
10. *Ibid.*, 47:30.

the hunter home from the hill": these beautiful lines by Robert Louis Stevenson contain more than a nostalgic note.

Occasionally, when I am at the airport, I happen to observe the loading of a double coffin, containing the body of a Jew who has lived, worked, raised children, prospered or failed, in the United States. It is being shipped for burial in the land of Abraham, Isaac and Jacob. The mystery of the origin apparently casts a spell even upon people who have few religious commitments. The modern secular Jew wants to rest in eternal peace, in proximity to the site where the patriarchs found their rest.

כי האדם עץ השדה לבא מפניך במצור. The man is indeed like the tree in the field. In this context, the verse should be interpreted as an affirmative statement,[11] not a rhetorical question. Man is indeed a rooted being, attached and committed to a homestead – no matter how far he may have traveled.

2

Both cosmos-conscious man and origin-conscious man quest for God, although they are not always aware of this quest. Man yearns for God, both in his feverish haste to get farther and farther from home, and in his lonesomeness for home and his experiencing the spell that home casts upon him. Cosmic man finds God (if ready for Him) in the vastness and boundlessness of the cosmic drama, in the heavenly galaxies billions of light years away. Home-bound, origin-minded man finds God in the limitedness and narrowness of finitude, in the smallness of the modest home into which man was born and to which he willy nilly returns. He discovers God in the origin, in the source, in the center of the burning bush.[12] Either infinity cannot

---

11. Following Ibn Ezra.
12. ... מתוך הסנה: שאל גוי אחד את ר"י בן קרחה מה ראה הקב"ה לדבר עם משה מתוך הסנה? א"ל ללמדך שאין מקום פנוי בלא שכינה אפילו סנה.

contain God, or God, if He so wills it, addresses man from the dimensionlessness of a point. What is the center of a bush if not a point! And out of that point, God spoke to Moses.

The wise King Solomon asked:

כי האמנם ישב אלקים על הארץ הנה השמים ושמי השמים לא יכלכלוך אף כי הבית הזה אשר בניתי.

But will God, in the very truth, dwell on the earth? Behold the heavens and the heavens of heavens cannot contain Thee; how much less this house that I have built.[13]

The logical answer to Solomon's question should have rendered the effort to construct a sanctuary futile, if not nonsensical. We would expect the wisest of all men, once having formulated this question, to regret the construction and call off the dedication festivities. Nevertheless, Solomon was not frightened by his question. He did dedicate the Sanctuary and did speak of it as the abode of the Almighty. Apparently God *does* descend from infinity to finitude, from boundlessness into the narrowness of the Sanctuary. The Midrash calls the awesome mystery of descent *tzimtzum*,[14] the mystery of God, the infinite, residing in finitude.

A Gentile asked R. Yehoshua b. Korhah: Why did God choose to speak with Moses from within the bramble bush? He answered: ... To teach you that there is no place devoid of *Shekhinah* (*Exodus Rabbah* 2).

13. I Kings 8:27.

14. בשעה שאמר הקב"ה למשה עשה לי משכן התחיל מתמיה ואומר כבודו של הקב"ה מלא עליונים ותחתונים והוא אומר עשה לי משכן... אמר הקב"ה לא כשם שאתה סבור כך אני סבור אלא כ' קרש בצפון וכ' בדרום וח' במערב ולא עוד אלא שארד ואצמצם שכינתי בתוך אמה על אמה.

When God told Moses to make Him a Sanctuary, Moses began to question, saying: "God's Glory is heaven and earth, yet He says – Make me a Sanctuary" ... Said God: "It is not as you think, but twenty planks in the north, twenty in the

Rabbi Joseph B. Soloveitchik

3

As we have stated above, cosmic man beholds the vision of God in infinity, in the endlessness of the distance which separates him from God, while origin-minded man experiences God in His closeness to man. As a rule, in times of joy and elation, one finds God's footsteps in the majesty and grandeur of the cosmos, in its vastness and its stupendous dynamics. When man is drunk with life, when he feels that living is a dignified affair, then man beholds God in infinity. In moments of ecstasy God addresses Himself to man through the twinkling stars and the roar of the endlessly distant heavens: ברכי נפשי את ה׳, ה׳ אלקי, גדלת מאד, הוד והדר לבשת, "O Lord my God Thou are very great, Thou are clothed with glory and majesty."[15] In such moments, *majestas Dei*, which not even the vast universe is large enough to accommodate, addresses itself to happy man.

However, with the arrival of the dark night of the soul, in moments of agony and black despair, when living becomes ugly and absurd, plainly nauseating, when man loses his sense of beauty and majesty, God addresses him, not from infinity but from the infinitesimal, not from the vast stretches of the universe but from a single spot in the darkness which surrounds suffering man, from within the black despair itself. Eleven years ago my wife lay on her deathbed and I watched her dying, day by day, hour by hour; medically, I could do very little for her, all I could do was to pray. However, I could not pray in the hospital; somehow I could not find God in the whitewashed, long corridors among the interns and the nurses. However, the need for prayer was great; I could not live without gratifying

---

south and eight in the west; moreover, I shall descend and *contract* my *Shekhinah* within one cubit by one" (*Exodus Rabbah* 34).

15. Psalms 104:1.

this need. The moment I returned home I would rush to my room, fall on my knees and pray fervently. God, in those moments, appeared not as the exalted, majestic King, but rather as a humble, close friend, brother, father: in such moments of black despair, He was not far from me; He was right there in the dark room; I felt His warm hand, כביכול, on my shoulder, I hugged His knees, כביכול. He was with me in the narrow confines of a small room, taking up no space at all. God's abiding in a fenced-in finite locus manifests His humility and love for man. In such moments *humilitas Dei*, which resides in the humblest and tiniest of places, addresses itself to man.[16]

4

The dual religious experience of *majestas* and *humilitas Dei* has had its impact upon Judaic morality. There are, indeed, as we have indicated above, two moralities: a morality of majesty and a morality of humility. The moral gesture of cosmic man aims at majesty or kingship. The highest moral achievement for cosmic man is sovereignty; man wants to be king. God is king of the world; man, imitating God, quests for kingship, not only over a limited domain, but over the far and distant regions of the cosmos, as well.[17] Man is summoned by God to be ruler, to be king, to be victorious. Victory, as the most important aspect of kingship, is an ethical goal and the human effort to achieve victory is a moral one, provided the means man employs are of a moral nature. To live, and to defy death, is a sublime moral achievement. That is why Judaism has displayed so much sympathy for scientific medicine and commanded the sick person to

---

16. See Exodus 20:2 and Rashi citing the Mekhilta.
17. In contradistinction to some Christian theologians, who look askance at man's attempts to reach the stars, Judaism is not only tolerant of these bold experiments, but indeed considers them to be ethically warranted.

seek medical help.[18] Curing, healing the sick is a divine attribute reflecting an activity (*rofe holim*) in which man ought to engage.

5

Underlying the ethic of victory is the mystical doctrine that creation is incomplete. God purposely left one aspect of creation unfinished in order to involve man in a creative gesture and to give him the opportunity to become both co-creator and king. The individual who is not engaged in the creative gesture can never be king; only a creator may lay claim to kingship and sovereignty. The creative gesture aims at the control and domination of a hostile environment. Under victory we understand, not only the subjection of nature to the needs of man, but also the establishment of a true and just society, and an equitable economic order.

6

This explains why the moral law was often identified, by cosmic man, with natural law. Surely, there is regularity in the natural universe. Why, asks cosmic man, should order not prevail in the human world as well? All the talk about natural law, which originated with the Stoa and found its philosophical formulation in Grotius' theory of *jus gentium*, has been indicative of cosmic man's approach to morality. In the opinion of cosmic man, morality must be intelligible and rational, appealing to the conscience and to the mind. Acceptance of *hukkim*, statutes which the *logos* cannot comprehend, is alien to the philosophy of cosmic man.

---

18. On the Jewish view of medicine, vide Nahmanides on Leviticus 26:11, and my discussion in "The Lonely Man of Faith" *Tradition* 7:2 (Summer 1965), footnote pp. 51–52 [*The Lonely Man of Faith*, Jerusalem: Maggid, 2012, pp. 59–60].

Majesty and Humility

Philosophical ethics, beginning with Plato and Aristotle and concluding with the pragmatic situational morality of today, is victory-minded and success-oriented. Man sets himself up as king and strives to triumph over opposition and hostility.

Judaism, however, knows that the kingship-victory morality is not always adequate. We said before that man meets God, not only in moments of joy and triumph, but also in times of disaster and distress, when God confronts him in the narrow straits of finitude, *min hametzar*, from out of the depths, *mima'amakim*. Then he encounters, not *majestas Dei* but *humilitas Dei*, God's glory compressed into the straits of the human finite destiny. It is self-evident that the humility-experience has to express itself in another set of ethical value judgments, in a unique morality. We do have two moralities, one of victory and triumph, one of withdrawal and retreat.

7

The ethic of retreat or withdrawal is rooted in the old mystery of *tzimtzum*, self-contraction, without which, not only the building of the Sanctuary, but even the creation of the world, would have been impossible. Reading the story of creation, a question arises in our minds: How can a finite world prevail beside God-infinity? From a mathematical point of view, infinity would swallow finitude: an infinite number plus a finite number equals infinity. The answer Lurianic Kabbalah offered is to be found again in the mystery of *tzimtzum*: the act of creation is identical with *tzimtzum* or withdrawal. God (metaphorically speaking) retreated in order to make room for a finite world. He created the world by engaging in a movement of recoil. For the sake of His love for man and for the world, God forsook infinity and stepped aside, *kivyakhol*.

Rabbi Joseph B. Soloveitchik

Let me ask the following question: Is this Lurianic doctrine of *tzimtzum* just a Kabbalistic mystery, without any moral relevance for us; or is it the very foundation of our morality? If God withdrew, and creation is a result of His withdrawal, then, guided by the principle of *imitatio Dei*, we are called upon to do the same. Jewish ethics, then, requires man, in certain situations, to withdraw.

Man must not always be victor. From time to time triumph should turn into defeat. Man, in Judaism, was created for both victory and defeat – he is both king and saint. He must know how to fight for victory and also how to suffer defeat. Modern man is frustrated and perplexed because he cannot take defeat. He is simply incapable of retreating humbly. Modern man boasts quite often that he has never lost a war. He forgets that defeat is built into the very structure of victory, that there is, in fact, no total victory; man is finite, so is his victory. Whatever is finite is imperfect; so is man's triumph.

8

In what areas of human endeavor does Judaism recommend self-defeat? Self-defeat is demanded in those areas in which man is most interested, where the individual expects to find the *summum bonum*, the realization of his most cherished dream or vision, where, in the opinion of pragmatic man, it is absolutely necessary for the individual to win, since losing the battle would mean total failure and frustration. It is precisely in those areas that God requires man to withdraw. God tells man to withdraw from whatever man desires the most. It is true of the father of the nation, as well as of plain ordinary people.

What was the most precious possession of Abraham; with what was he concerned the most? Isaac. Because the son meant so much to him, God instructed him to retreat, to give the son

Majesty and Humility

away: קח נא את בנך את יחידך אשר אהבת את יצחק, "Take your son, your only son, whom you love – Isaac."[19]

What of the ordinary person? Is there, for example, a more sensitive area in the lives of two young people – man and woman – than their love-relationship? Therefore, the principle of self-defeating action must govern the relationship in this area. Sex, if unredeemed, may turn into a brutal, ugly performance which man shares with the beast. Sex, therefore, is in need of redemption. It must be purged of its coarseness and animality. What action did Judaism recommend to man in order to achieve this purpose? The movement of withdrawal and self-defeat. Only in light of this principle can we begin to understand many of the strict Halachic rules of separation.[20]

What does man cherish more than the intellect, around which his sense of dignity is centered? Precisely because of the supremacy of the intellect in human life, the Torah requires, at times, the suspension of the authority *logos*. Man defeats himself by accepting norms that the intellect cannot assimilate into its normative system. The Judaic concept of *hok* represents human surrender and human defeat. Man, an intellectual being, ignores the *logos* and burdens himself with laws whose rational motif he cannot grasp. He withdraws from the rationalistic position. In a word, withdrawal is required, in all areas of human experience and endeavor; whatever is most significant, whatever attracts man the most, must be given up.

What happens after man makes this movement of recoil and retreats? God may instruct him to resume his march to victory and move onward in conquest and triumph. The movement of recoil redeems the forward-movement, and the readiness to

---

19. Genesis 22:2.
20. Vide "Catharsis" for an elaboration of the principle of self-defeat.

accept defeat purges the uncontrollable lust for victory. Once man has listened and retreated, he may later be instructed to march straight to victory.

Abraham was told to withdraw, and to defeat himself, by giving Isaac away. He listened; God accepted Isaac but did not retain him. God returned him to Abraham: וירש זרעך את שער אויביו, "And thy seed shall take possession of his enemies' gate."[21] Abraham found victory in retreat.[22]

---

21. Genesis 22:17.
22. Moses was less fortunate. He withdrew; he gazed upon the land from afar; but his prayers were not fulfilled. He never entered the Promised Land, which was only half a mile away. He listened, though his total obedience did not result in victory. God's will is inscrutable.

Catharsis

The Halacha has never despaired of man, either as a natural being integrated into his physical environment, or as a spiritual personality confronting God.

This sufferance of man on the part of the Halacha is not an unqualified one. The Halacha demands that man purge himself in order to achieve his full worth. Isaiah, describing the future redemption of Israel, speaks of purgation as an indispensable condition of redemption: ואשיבה ידי עליך ואצרף כבר סיגך, "I shall cleanse thy dross as with soap."[1] Similarly, our Rabbis have stated repeatedly that the purpose which Torah and *mitzvot* pursue is that of purification of the human being.[2] In other

---

This essay was delivered at the Fourteenth Morris Burg Memorial Lecture at M.I.T., under the aegis of the B'nai Brith Hillel Foundation, on November 18, 1962.
1. Isaiah 1:25.
2. Witness the following Midrashic statement:

רב אמר לא נתנו המצות אלא לצרף בהן את הבריות.
וכי מה איכפת ליה להקב״ה למי ששוחט מן הצואר או מי ששוחט מן העורף?
הוי לא נתנו המצוות אלא לצרף בהן את הבריות.

Rabbi Joseph B. Soloveitchik

words, catharsis is a *sine qua non* for a meaningful existence which Halacha approves.

What did Halacha understand under catharsis or purging? The analysis of a liturgical text will help us answer this question. Among the several benedictions comprising the *birkot hashahar* which we pronounce daily, thanking the Almighty for restoring us, each morning, to a full and active life, we recite two benedictions which, *prima facie*, appear to be synonymous and therefore redundant. One benediction reads *ozer Yisrael bigevurah*, in standard translation, "who girds Israel with might"; and the other one, *hanoten layaef koah*, "who gives strength to the weary."[3] Apparently our liturgists discriminated semantically between *koah* and *gevurah* (strength and might). Had they considered the two terms fully synonymous, they would not have formulated two benedictions; one would have sufficed.

What does *koah* mean? *Koah* denotes any aptitude which God has bestowed upon man at birth. The term *koah* denotes primarily physical strength, the capability of performing work which requires an unusual amount of physical vigor. This is the dominant meaning of the word in the Bible.[4]

Koah, as such, is not an exclusively human category, since it is related, in most of its aspects, to man's capabilities as a natural being. The beast shares with man all his organic aptitudes. Thus the category of *koah* is applicable to man and beast alike.

Rav said: "The *mitzvot* were not given but to purge men. For what difference is there for God if one slaughters from the neck, or slaughters from the nape? Say rather that the *mitzvot* were given in order to purge men" (*Genesis Rabbah* 44).

3. *Ozer Yisrael bigevurah* is one of the blessings enumerated in the Talmud (*Brakhot* 60b); the earliest clear reference to *hanoten layaef koah* is medieval (vide *Tur* and *Shulhan Arukh, Orah Hayyim*, sec. 46 and commentators *ad loc.*).

4. In later Hebrew, this basic meaning is expanded to include the senses (e.g. *koah hare'iyah* = sense of sight; *koah hashemi'ah* = hearing).

Koah is not a unique gift bestowed by the Creator upon man. It is rather an integral part of the unbroken uniform functionality of a natural universe.

What is *gevurah*? *Gevurah*, in contradistinction to *koah*, is an exclusive grant of God to man which demonstrates the latter's unique position in creation – man's charismatic endowment and his chosenness. Man, as a brute existing in the realm of immediate mechanical, uninterrupted life functions, was furnished with *koah*. Man as a personality distinct and different from the beast and fowl of the field, who confronts nature in a reflective, inquisitive mood, possesses the quality of *gevurah*;[5] this he shares with no one.[6]

2

Gevurah, in the context of the Biblical narrative and hymn, denotes the capacity of attaining victory, of defeating a foe who engages one in combat. The Scriptures use this term almost exclusively with respect to the exploits of the warrior – the victor. It refers to combat, and signifies successful action taken by one of the combatants.

The victory with which *gevurah* is identified is not military victory alone, or indeed any triumph which is merely the result of superior manpower and materials. On the contrary, at times the combatant who is defeated on the field of battle is the one who emerges as the *gibbor*, victor in a higher historical sense;

---

5. Apparent exceptions to this rule are to be understood either as figurative usage (e.g. Proverbs 30:30) or as elliptical formulations (e.g. Psalms 147:10, where the Psalmist refers to the *gevurah* of the horse's *rider*).
6. Both attributes, *koah* and *gevurah*, were applied to the Almighty, *kivyakhol*, since He is both the source of cosmic dynamics (*koah*: e.g. Isaiah 40:26; Nahum 1:3) and the source of the charismatic human heroic gesture (*gevurah*: Deuteronomy 10:17).

and not the apparent winner.⁷ *Gevurah* is sometimes inversely related to *koah*, to the degree of might man has at his disposal. The greater the force one wields, the less *gevurah* one needs to display. Conversely, the weaker one is, the tougher the odds, the more exalted is the action of the *gibbor*, which disregards practical reasoning and resorts to "the absurd."

Thus, a new element is introduced into the gesture of *gevurah*, namely, heroism or action undertaken contrary to human logic and human practical judgment. This kind of action quite often leads to ultimate victory. There are situations in life with which clear-cut logical processes and utilitarian approaches fail to cope, while the sudden spontaneous leap into the absurd (to use a Kierkegaardian phrase) may save man when he finds himself in utter distress. This non-rational and impractical action is heroic, and is identical with *gevurah*.

3

ויאמר לא יעקב יאמר עוד שמך כי אם ישראל כי שרית עם אלקים ועם אנשים ותוכל.

---

7. The Talmud (*Yoma* 69b) explains why the Men of the Great Assembly (*Anshei Knesset Hagedolah*) received this appellation:

> משה אמר הא-ל הגדול הגבור... אתא דניאל אמר נכרים משתעבדים בבניו, איה גבורותיו? לא אמר גבור... אתו אינהו ואמרו אדרבה זו היא גבורת גבורתו שכובש את יצרו שנותן ארך אפים לרשעים.

> Moses said: "The great God, the *gibbor*" (Deuteronomy 10:17) ... Came Daniel and said: Foreigners subjugate His sons; where is His *gevurah*? He did not say *gibbor*.... The Men of the Great Assembly came and said: Precisely that is His *gevurah*, that He overcomes His anger and is patient with the wicked.

> Did not the Men of the Great Assembly interpret *gibbor* and *gevurah* in terms of the heroic gesture, which defies *koah* and makes the impossible a reality? These great men identified *gevurah* with withdrawal and defeat.

Catharsis

> Thy name shall no more be called Jacob, but Israel, for thou hast striven with God and with man and thou hast prevailed.[8]

Jacob had emerged victorious from a most awesome encounter; he had held fast his mysterious foe, through a night of sorrow, fear and loneliness, until the new day dawned. Was Jacob's victory something to be expected; could it have been predicted logically? Was he certain of victory? Of course not. He was alone, weak and unarmed, a novice in the art of warfare. His antagonist was a powerful professional warrior. Why did Jacob not surrender to the foe who attacked him in the dark? Jacob acted "absurdly," and contrary to all rational practical considerations. In other words, he acted heroically. He, the lonely and helpless Jacob, dared to engage a mighty adversary in combat. He, who had displayed so much business acumen and the keenness of a pragmatic mind during his long sojourn in Laban's household, suddenly, in the darkness of a grisly, strange night, made the leap into the "absurd." He refused to yield to a superior force and declared war upon an invincible enemy. What Jacob manifested was not *koah* but *gevurah*, heroism, which is always employed when reason despairs and logic retreats. With daybreak, the helpless, lonely, non-logical Jacob, found himself, unexpectedly, the victor, the hero.

The impossible and absurd had triumphed over the possible and logical: heroism, not logic, won the day. Is this merely the story of one individual's experience? Is it not in fact the story of *Knesset Israel*, an entity which is engaged in an "absurd" struggle for survival thousands of years?

---

8. Genesis 32:29.

Rabbi Joseph B. Soloveitchik

4

At this point we may note that the narrative about Jacob is *toto genere* different from the classical epic. For classical man heroism was intrinsically an aesthetic category which fascinated man with its grandeur and glory. The classical man was an aesthete, endowed with a demonic quality; he longed for vastness. His creative fantasy was boundless and reached for the impossible. He suffered from a sense of frustration and disenchantment; since no man, not even the most accomplished aesthete, can ever cross the Rubicon separating finitude from infinity. In his agony the classical aesthete invented the image of the hero. The mere myth of the hero gave the aesthete endless comfort. At least, the classical aesthete said to himself, there was an individual who dared to do the impossible and to achieve the grandiose. In short, the hero of classical man was the grandiose figure with whom, in order to satisfy his endless vanity, classical man identified himself: hero worship is basically self-worship. The classical idea of heroism, which is aesthetic in its very essence, lacks the element of absurdity and is intrinsically dramatic and theatrical.[9] The hero is an actor who performs in order to impress an appreciative audience. The crowd cheers, the chronicler records, countless generations afterwards admire, bards and minstrels sing of the hero. The classical heroic gesture represents, as I said before, frightened, disenchanted man, who tries to achieve immortality and permanence by identifying himself with the heroic figure on the stage. It does not represent a way of life. It lasts for a while, vibrant and forceful, but soon man reverts to the non-heroic mood of everyday living.

---

9. For Aristotle, in his *Poetics*, the theme of tragedy is the noble, impressive action, and its function is the catharsis of the emotions of *eleos* and *phobos* (pity and terror), in other words, the pleasurable relief of the audience, its liberation from emotion.

Catharsis

In contrast to classical aesthetic heroism, Biblical heroism, as portrayed in the narrative about Jacob, is not nurtured by an ephemeral mood or a passing state of mind. It is perhaps the central motif in our existential experience. It pervades the human mind steadily, and imparts to man a strange feeling of tranquility. The heroic person, according to our view, does not succumb to frenzy and excitement. Biblical heroism is not ecstatic but rather contemplative; not loud but hushed; not dramatic or spectacular but mute. The individual, instead of undertaking heroic action sporadically, lives constantly as a hero. Jacob did not just act heroically upon the spur of the moment. His action was indicative of a resolute way of life; he was not out to impress anybody. This type of heroics lasts as long as man is aware of himself as a singular being.

5

Jacob was victorious at daybreak when the mist began to lift. His adversary was defeated and Jacob was ready to consummate his victory. The mysterious enemy was at Jacob's mercy. All Jacob had to do in order to bring the engagement to a successful conclusion was to destroy his antagonist and thus eliminate the threat of another attack. Jacob acted differently, and contrary to what others in his place would have done; when the moment at which Jacob could enjoy his victory arrived, he released the attacker and set him free. What motivated such an act? Of course, the antagonist had pleaded with him. He had begged for his freedom: ויאמר שלחני כי עלה השחר, "Release me, for the morning star hath risen."[10] But why did Jacob listen to the plea of a man who, a short while ago, had been determined to annihilate him? The vanquished adversary did not

---

10. Genesis 32:27.

even promise Jacob that he would not repeat his attack. To release such a dangerous fiend was "unreasonable." This very unreasonableness endowed the act with the quality of the heroic, and may serve as a pattern for Halachic heroism.

6

What is heroism in the Halacha? What does the Halacha recommend to us, that we may attain heroic stature? The answer is: one must perform the dialectical movement. The Halachic catharsis expresses itself in paradoxical movement in two opposite directions – in surging forward boldly and in retreating humbly. Man's heroic experience is a polar, antithetic one. Man drives forward only to retreat and to reverse, subsequently, the direction of his movement.

The Torah wants man, who is bold and adventurous in his quest for opportunities, to act heroically, and at the final moment, when it appears to him that victory is within reach, to stop short, turn around, and retreat. At the most exalted moment of triumph and fulfillment man must forego the ecstasy of victory and take defeat at his own hands. Jacob acted in this manner; he engaged in the dialectical performance. He did not consummate his victory; instead, he set free the antagonist whom he had defeated and whom he could have destroyed. By freeing the defeated enemy Jacob defeated himself. He withdrew from a position he had won through courage and fortitude. He engaged in the movement of recoil.

II

Halacha teaches that at every level of our total existential experience – the aesthetic-hedonic, the emotional, the intellectual, the moral-religious – one must engage in the dialectical movement by alternately advancing and retreating. The

Catharsis

Halacha was cognizant of the program the Creator set for man: ויברך אתם אלקים וכו' ומלאו את הארץ וכבשֻהָ, "Replenish the earth and subdue it."[11] Man was called upon to defy opposition on the part of nature and to march to victory. Biblical man is out to subdue his environment. Yet, when conquest is within man's reach and the road to realization has been cleared of all hindrances, man-victor, who needs only to reach out and grab everything his heart has anxiously desired, must change his course and begin to withdraw. When victory is near, man must invite defeat and surrender the spoils that he had quested for so long. The movement is dialectical: forward-marching ends in retreat, which, in turn, leads to a resumption of the forward-march. After man withdraws from the position which he has acquired through hard labor and sacrifice, he begins once again to swing forward. Again Halacha encourages man to pursue greatness, vastness, to experiment daringly with his liberties, to search feverishly for dominion. And again, Halacha will command man to halt, and to make an about-face. This dialectical movement, no matter how incomprehensible to modern man, forms, as we stated above, the very heart of Halachic living. In a word, the Halacha teaches man how to conquer and how to lose, how to seize initiative and how to renounce, how to succeed, how to invite defeat, and how to resume the striving for victory.

I

The idea of catharsis through the dialectical movement manifests itself in all Halachic norms regulating human life. Nowhere, however, does this doctrine of dialectical catharsis assert itself more frequently than it does in the aesthetic-hedonic realm.

---

11. *Ibid.*, 1:28.

How does man purge himself in this realm? By engaging in the dialectical movement, by withdrawing, at the moment when passion reaches its peak. The stronger the grip of the physiological drive is felt by man, the more intoxicating and bewildering the prospect of hedonic gratification, the greater the redemptive capacity of the dialectical catharsis – of the movement of recoil.

"בטנך ערמת חטים סוגה בשושנים״ - אדם נושא אשה בן ל׳ שנה בן מ׳ שנה, משמוציא יציאותיו הוא בא לזקק לה והיא אומרת לו כשושנה אדומה ראיתי ופורש ממנה מיד. מי גרם לו שלא יקרב לה, איזה כותל ברזל יש ביניהם ואיזה עמוד ברזל ביניהם, אי זה נחש נשכו, איזה עקרב עקצו שלא יקרב לה? דברי תורה שרכין כשושנה שנא׳ בה ״ואל אשה בנדת טומאתה לא תקרב״. וכן מי שהביאו לו תמחוי של חתיכות, אמרו לו חלב נפל שם ומשך ידו ולא טעמו. מי גרם לו שלא לטעום, איזה נחש נשכו שלא יטעום ואיזה עקרב עקצו שלא יקרב ויטעם ויטעם אותם? דברי תורה שרכין כשושנה שכתוב בה ״כל חלב וכל דם לא תאכלו״.

"Thy belly is like a heap of wheat set about with lilies." It often happens that a man takes a wife when he is thirty or forty years of age. When, after going to great expense, he wishes to associate with her, and she says to him, "I have seen a rose-red speck," he immediately recoils. What made him retreat and keep away from her? Was there an iron fence, did a serpent bite him, did a scorpion sting him? … A dish of meat is placed before a man and he is told some forbidden fat has fallen into it. He withdraws his hand from the food. What stopped him from tasting it? Did a serpent bite him; did a scorpion sting him? Only the words of the Torah, which are as soft as a bed of lilies.[12]

---

12. *Shir ha Shirim R.* to Song 7:3.

Catharsis

Bride and bridegroom are young, physically strong and passionately in love with each other. Both have patiently waited for this rendezvous to take place. Just one more step and their love would have been fulfilled, a vision realized. Suddenly the bride and groom make a movement of recoil. He, gallantly, like a chivalrous knight, exhibits paradoxical heroism. He takes his own defeat. There is no glamor attached to his withdrawal. The latter is not a spectacular gesture, since there are no witnesses to admire and to laud him. The heroic act did not take place in the presence of jubilating crowds; no bards will sing of these two modest, humble young people. It happened in the sheltered privacy of their home, in the stillness of the night. The young man, like Jacob of old, makes an about-face; he retreats at the moment when fulfillment seems assured.

This kind of divine dialectical discipline is not limited to man's sexual life, but extends to all areas of natural drive and temptation. The hungry person must forego the pleasure of taking food, no matter how strong the temptation; men of property must forego the pleasure of acquisition, if the latter is Halachically and morally wrong. In a word, Halacha requires of man that he possess the capability of withdrawal.[13] Of course, as we have made evident above, man is called, following the movement of withdrawal, to advance once again, toward full victory.

2

The Torah demanded cathartic action, not only in the hedonic, but in the emotional world of man, as well. In the carnal hedonic realm, catharsis expresses itself in the movement of recoil from something extraneous; e.g. the retreat of the bridegroom from the bride, or the renunciation of food by the

---

13. איזהו גבור? הכובש את יצרו!: Who is a *gibbor*? He who conquers his drives (*Avot* 4:1).

hungry man. In the emotional sphere, however, the cathartic act consists in retreating or disengaging from oneself, from one's own inner world, in renouncing something that is a part of oneself, such as a sentiment, a mood or a state of mind. Can we indeed withdraw from ourselves, rejecting the feeling which grips us with enormous force, dismissing an experience which at times is overpowering? Halacha says yes. The Torah formulated laws governing the deeds of man, such as "thou shalt not murder," "thou shalt not bear false witness." It has also tried to control the inner life of man. Laws such as "thou shalt not covet," "thou shalt not hate thy brother," are as integral a part of the Halachic normative system as are those related to human external action. In a word, the Halacha thinks there is an ethic, not only of action, but of feeling, as well. Man is master over his own emotional world, capable of disowning feelings or emotions, however compulsive or powerful, if they seem to be disruptive; and, conversely, of assimilating redemptive emotion into his personality. Catharsis in the emotional sphere, according to Halacha, consists in active human interference with the emotive experience.

    Let me illustrate the Halachic idea of inner withdrawal or emotional catharsis. Aaron the high priest met with disaster. On the most joyous day of his life, when the Tabernacle was dedicated and he was inaugurated into his office, two of his sons died. Death is always the great evil which man cannot accept. It is certainly unacceptable to a father whose grief over the loss of a son is limitless. How much more so the unreasonable death of two sons, who had entered the sanctuary to worship and to serve the Lord and were devoured by a fire from the Lord. Moses addressed the following words to Aaron immediately after the disaster struck:

ויאמר משה וכו' ראשיכם אל תפרעו ובגדיכם לא תפרמו ולא תמתו ועל כל העדה יקצף, ואחיכם כל בית ישראל יבכו את השרפה אשר שרף ה'. ומפתח אהל מועד לא תצאו פן תמתו כי שמן משחת ה' עליכם.

Let not the hair on your head go loose, neither rend your garments; lest ye die, lest wrath come upon all the people. But let your brethren, the whole house of Israel, bewail the burning which the Lord hath kindled. Ye shall not go out from the door of the Tabernacle, lest ye die; for the anointing oil of the Lord is upon you.[14]

Moses enjoined Aaron and his children from mourning for Nadav and Avihu. Aaron and his two surviving sons were enjoined from shedding a tear for them. Why? Because the priests constituted a community of the anointed who were consecrated exclusively to the service of the Lord. The inalienable right, to which every parent is entitled, of mourning the death of a child was denied to Aaron and his sons. The commitment or consecration of a priest to God is ultimate, all-demanding, and all-inclusive. God lays unrestricted claim not to a part but to the whole of the human personality. Existence *in toto*, in its external and inward manifestations, is consecrated to God. Aaron belonged to no one, not even to himself, but to God. Therefore he was not even free to give himself over to the grief precipitated by the loss of his two sons; he had no private world of his own. Even the heart of Aaron was divine property.

What does all this mean in psychological terms? God wanted Aaron to disown the strongest emotion in man – the

---

14. Leviticus 10:6-7.

love for a child. Is it possible? As far as modern man is concerned I would not dare answer. With respect to Biblical man we read that Aaron acted in accord with the divine instruction: ויעשו כדבר משה, "And they did so, according to Moses' word."[15] Aaron withdrew from himself; he withdrew from being a father. This kind of movement of recoil is tantamount to self-denial. Such action is certainly cathartic, because it is certainly heroic; as such it is far more exalted than the aesthetic Aristotelian catharsis, which Judaism did not accept.

Not only Aaron, but the entire covenantal community, was summoned by God into His service. Once man enters the service of God, be it as high-priest, be it as an ordinary humble person, his commitment is not partial; it is total. He is subject to the divine call for total inner withdrawal. Here the Halacha intervenes frequently in the most intimate and personal phases of our lives and makes demands upon us which often impress the uninitiated as overly rigid and formal.

Let us take an example. We all know the law that a festival suspends the mourning for one of the seven intimate relatives. If one began to observe the *shiva* period a short time before the holiday was ushered in, the commencement of the latter cancels the *shiva*. Let us not forget that *avelut* (mourning) in Halacha consists of more than the performance of external ritual or ceremony. It is far more than that. It is an inner experience of black despair, of complete existential failure, of the absurdity of being. It is a grisly experience which overwhelms man, which shatters his faith and exposes his I-awareness as a delusion. Similarly, the precept of *simhat yom tov* (to rejoice on a holiday) includes, not only ceremonial actions, but a genuine experience of joy, as well. When the Torah decreed ושמחת בחגך,

---

15. *Ibid.*

Catharsis

"and thou shalt rejoice in thy feast,"[16] it referred, not to merrymaking and entertaining, to artificial gaiety or some sort of shallow hilarity, but to an all-penetrating depth-experience of spiritual joy, serenity and peace of mind deriving from faith and the awareness of God's presence. Now let us visualize the following concrete situation. The mourner, who has buried a beloved wife or mother, returns home from the graveyard where he has left part of himself, where he has witnessed the mockery of human existence. He is in a mood to question the validity of our entire axiological universe. The house is empty, dreary; every piece of furniture reminds the mourner of the beloved person he has buried. Every corner is full of memories. Yet the Halacha addresses itself to the lonely mourner, whispering to him: "Rise from your mourning; cast the ashes from your head; change your clothes; light the festive candles; recite over a cup of wine the *Kiddush* extolling the Lord for giving us festivals of gladness and sacred seasons of joy; pronounce the blessing of *Sheheheyanu*: 'Blessed art Thou...who has kept us in life and has preserved us and has enabled us to reach this season'; join the jubilating community and celebrate the holiday as if nothing had transpired, as if the beloved person over whose death you grieve were with you." The Halacha, which at times can be very tender, understanding and accommodating, may, on other occasions, act like a disciplinarian demanding obedience. The Halacha suggests to man, broken in body and spirit, carrying the burden of an absurd existence, that he change his mood, that he cast off his grief and choose joy. Let us repeat the question: Is such a metamorphosis of the state of mind of an individual possible? Can one make the leap from utter bleak desolation and hopelessness into joyous trust? Can one replace the experience of

---

16. Deuteronomy 16:14.

monstrosity with the feeling of highest meaningfulness? I have no right to judge. However, I know of people who attempted to perform this greatest of all miracles.

This leap is certainly heroic. It is less spectacular than the death of an Achilles; yet it is more heroic, more redeeming, because it is performed in humility and in the hush of a dark night of loneliness.

3

Judaism insisted upon catharsis in another area, namely, the intellectual. Judaism insisted upon the redeeming of the *logos* and maintained that there is an unredeemed cognitive gesture, just as there is an unredeemed carnal drive. When I say there is an unredeemed cognitive gesture, I do not refer to mythical thinking, which is not guided by scientific method and precision, but to the most modern system of scientific inquiry. The latter may be considered unredeemed if the scientist does not subject his cognitive act to an extraneous catharsis, which consists in the dialectical movement: marching forward, inspired by victory, and retracing one's steps in defeat.

Let me explain: when I speak of cognitive withdrawal or self-negation, I do not mean to suggest that the scientist should conduct his inquiry without thoroughness or inconclusively. On the contrary, every scholar is guided intuitively by an ethical norm, which tells him to search the truth assiduously and not to rest until he has it within his reach. Cognitive withdrawal is related, not to the scientific inquiry as a logical operation, but rather to the axiological experience of scientific work. Knowing is not an impersonal performance which can be computerized, emptied of its rich, colorful, experiential content. It is, instead, an integral part of the knower as a living person, with all his complex emotional experiences and axiological judgments.

Catharsis

Next to the religious experience, knowledge is perhaps the most vibrant and resonant personal experience. It sweeps the whole of the personality, sometimes like a gentle wave infusing the knower with a sense of tranquility and serenity; at other times like a mighty onrushing tide, arousing the soul to its depth and raising it to a pitch of ecstasy. As we have said before, the catharsis of knowledge refers to something which takes place, not within the formal logical realm, but within the experiential.

Cognitive catharsis consists in discovering the unknowability of being. Commitment to knowledge, to scientific inquiry, implies, *ipso facto*, the recognition of the eternal mystery, which grows with the advance of knowledge, which deepens with the triumphant march of the human mind, and which becomes, with every cognitive breakthrough, more baffling, perplexing and challenging. Often we raise a Kohelet-type question: is man indeed a knower? For man always faces the paradoxical situation of solving one problem, only to discover another problem, more complex and inclusive than the first, and which has been precipitated by the very solution to the old problem.

Furthermore, man discovers that the scientific gesture and the *mysterium magnum* belong to different realms. Science explores a world of its own making – a world of relational constructs and freely-created conceptual series. The *mysterium magnum*, which is imbedded in our qualitative environment consisting of sound, color, touch, fragrance, sensations of heat, moisture and the like, can never be subjected to scientific interpretation and elucidation. What the scientist does is not to explain the qualitative phenomena but to create a parallel quantitative order of abstract mathematical correlates which he manipulates with great freedom, since they are ultimately creations of his own mind. There is no scientific explanation of our real problem: what is the essence of the qualitative world we live in? There is, to be sure, a creative duplication which serves well, so far as technology is concerned, and which gradually places our environment under human control. However, the lanes of creation which we sense, feel, enjoy and fear, in which we are enmeshed, body and soul – these remain uncharted. Hence, the cognitive experience contains not only the rapture of knowing but also the terror and awe of the great mystery of the strange and uninterpretable being, namely, the universe as a qualitative rather than a quantitative entity.

If the scholar, simultaneously with the ecstasy of knowing, experiences also the agony of confusion, and together with the sweetness of triumph over Being, feels the pain and despair of defeat by Being, then his cognitive gesture is purged and redeemed. Then, and only then, does this gesture become heroic. Then, and only then, is the scientific experience a humble and not an arrogant one.

Catharsis requires of the scientist two basic admissions. First, as we have already pointed out above, that he may, at best, attain knowledge and understanding of the cosmic process when the latter is translated into quantitative abstract constructs. However, he must recognize that the human mind will never comprehend the link between the mathematical idea and the event, between the formula, which is a product of the mind, and the behavioral patterns of organic and inorganic matter. Second, the moral law can never be legislated in ultimate terms by the human mind. Any attempt on the part of scientific research, no matter how progressive, to replace the moral law engraved by the Divine hand on the two stone tablets of Sinai with man-made rules of behavior, is illegitimate. Adam tried to legislate the moral norm; he was driven from Paradise. In our day, modern man is engaged in a similar undertaking, which demonstrates pride and arrogance, and is doomed to failure.

Catharsis

4

Man must be ready to accept defeat not only in the carnal-aesthetic, emotional, or intellectual world but also in the moral-religious world, in his relationship with God.[17] Man must be capable of recognizing that he is subject, willy-nilly, to the dialectical movement even in his encounter with God, even when he is certain that God is close to him and all he has to do is to make the final leap into the embrace of his Maker. There is an unredeemed moral and religious experience, as there is an unredeemed body and an unredeemed *logos*. Let us be candid: if one has not redeemed his religious life, he may become self-righteous, insensitive, or even destructive. The story of the Crusades, the Inquisition and other outbursts of religious fanaticism bear out this thesis. Judaism has sanctioned man, has stated that there is a spark of divinity in man; Judaism has never subscribed to the philosophy that man is intrinsically sinful. On the contrary, we have taught that the moral challenge which confronts man and the opportunities offered him are unlimited. Man, as seen by Judaism, is potentially a good, progressive being. However, man often finds himself in the grip of an overwhelming, irresistible force that pulls him downward. The ascent up the mount of the Lord often turns into a rapid descent down the mount. The impetuous and passionate rush toward God may suddenly become a flight from God. Man moves toward the fulfillment of his destiny along a zig-zag line – progress frequently superseded by retrogression; closeness to God, by the dark night of separation. Man not only rises but falls as well; and rises again from his fall only to fall once more. Moral erring and culpability are

---

17. Withdrawal, in the moral-religious sphere, differs from, withdrawal in other areas. While, in other areas, the Torah requires of man that he withdraw voluntarily from certain positions he conquered, in the moral-religious sphere withdrawal is identical with the awareness of imperfection and sin.

Rabbi Joseph B. Soloveitchik

interwoven into our very existential fabric. No man can claim that he is perfect, that his existential experience has been purged of all selfish, undignified, brutish motives. In a word, the Bible is confident of man, but it is also very suspicious of man. Catharsis of religious life consists exactly in the awareness of the long interludes during which man finds himself at an infinite distance from God: the periodic states of ecstasy engendered by the feeling of closeness to God alternate with the states of black despair, which even the prophet encounters during moments of exile from the presence of the Almighty. Those long periods of black despair (*hester panim*) contain the cathartic element which cleanses and redeems religious life. The breaking of the covenantal tablets is an experience every committed individual must endure. Only after Moses had lost everything he was questing for, did he ascend Mount Sinai to receive, not only two new tablets of stone, but also the radiant countenance and the great mission of transmitting and teaching Torah to the covenantal community. On the long life journey, at one point or another, one must reach the absurd stage at which one finds oneself bankrupt and forlorn. The Bible, with ruthless honesty, recorded such experiences of failure in the lives of our greatest. Man must be cognizant of this tragic fact, which sooner or later he must encounter, if his metaphysical destiny is to be realized.

Great is not the man who has never faltered but the man who tripped, fell and rose again to greater heights.[18] Sin is a reality, not just a potential threat. Perfect man has never been created.[19] If a man is not conscious of the contradiction inherent in the very core of his personality, he lives in the world of illusion and leads an unredeemed existence. It matters not what

---

18. Vide Maimonides' *Eight Chapters*, Ch. 6.
19. Vide Ecclesiastes 7:20.

Catharsis

we call such a complacent state of mind – self-righteousness, pride, haughtiness, stupidity – it is all a manifestation of a brutish and raw state of mind.

At this point, the idea of *teshuva* emerges and conveys to man the message of catharsis. In what does this catharsis express itself? In the aptitude of man to take a critical look at himself and to admit failure, in the courage to confess, to plead guilty, in the readiness to accept defeat. The outcry of Judah, the outcry of aristocrat and judge, who admitted that he was wrong and the poor harlot was right – ויכר יהודה ויאמר צדקה ממני, "She has been more righteous than I"[20] – was the great cathartic act, which cleansed him and redeemed his life. To recite *viddui*, a confession, is the greatest of all virtues, the most heroic act; it is catharsis *par excellence*.

הגיד לך אדם מה טוב ומה ה' דורש ממך כי אם עשות משפט ואהבת חסד והצנע לכת עם אלקיך.

He hath showed thee, man, what is good and that doth the Lord require of thee, but to do justly and to love mercy, and to walk humbly with thy God.[21]

In paraphrase I would say: He showed thee, man, what is good, and what doth the Lord require of thee, but to move forward boldly, to triumph over and to subdue thy environment, and to retreat humbly when victory is within thy grasp.

---

20. Genesis 38:26.
21. Micah 6:8.

Redemption, Prayer, Talmud Torah

Redemption is a fundamental category in Judaic historical thinking and experiencing. Our history was initiated by a Divine act of redemption and, we are confident, will reach its finale in a Divine act of *ultimate* redemption.

I

What is redemption?

Redemption involves a movement by an individual or a community from the periphery of history to its center; or, to employ a term from physics, redemption is a centripetal movement. To be on the periphery means to be a non-history-making entity, while movement toward the center renders the same entity history-making and history-conscious. Naturally the question arises: What is meant by a history-making people

---

This essay was delivered at a faculty colloquium at the University of Pennsylvania, under the aegis of the B'nai Brith Hillel Foundation, May, 1973.

or community? A history-making people is one that leads a speaking, story-telling, communing, free existence, while a non-history-making, non-history-involved group leads a non-communing and therefore a silent, unfree existence.

2

Like redemption, prayer too is a basic experiential category in Judaism. We have appeared, within the historical arena, as a prayerful nation. Abraham, Isaac, Jacob, Moses, David and Solomon all prayed. Through prayer they achieved the covenant with God, and through prayer, we expect eventually to realize that covenant.

The Halacha has viewed prayer and redemption as two inseparable ideas. The Halacha requires that the Silent Prayer (*Amida*) be preceded, without a break, by the benediction of *Gaal Yisrael*, which proclaims God as the Redeemer of Israel.[1]

What motivated the Halacha to link prayer with redemption? Apparently our Sages considered prayer and redemption to be structurally identical. Of what does this identity consist? In order to answer this question, it would be profitable to subject both ideas to precise phenomenological analysis.

3

Redemption, we have stated, is identical with communing, or with the revelation of the word, i.e., the emergence of speech. When a people leaves a mute world and enters a world of sound, speech and song, it becomes a redeemed people, a free people.

---

[1]. אמר ר׳ יוחנן איזהו בן העולם הבא זה הסומך גאולה לתפלה.
R. Yohanan said: "Who has a share in the World to Come? He who adjoins the blessing of *Gaal Yisrael* to the Silent Prayer." (*Brakhot* 4b)

Redemption, Prayer, Talmud Torah

In other words, a mute life is identical with bondage; a speech-endowed life is a free life.

The slave lives in silence,[2] if such a meaningless existence may be called life. He has no message to deliver. In contrast with the slave, the free man bears a message, has a good deal to tell, and is eager to convey his life story to anyone who cares to listen. No wonder the Torah has, four times, emphasized the duty of the father – a liberated slave – to tell his children, born into freedom, the story of his liberation.[3] Free man, who is eager to tell his story, is always surrounded by an audience willing to listen to his story. The slave has neither a story nor a curious audience. Moreover, he is not merely a speechless being, but a mute being, devoid not only of the word, but of the meaningful sound as well.

4

What is responsible for the dumbness of the slave? The lack of a basic experience, namely that of suffering or distress, which is perhaps the most central aspect of the human I-awareness.

Suffering is not pain. Though colloquially the two words are used as synonyms, they signify two different experiences. Pain is a natural sensation, a physiological reaction of the organism to any kind of abnormality or tissue pathology. It is, as Aristotle already knew, a built-in mechanical signal that warns man whenever his physical existence is menaced from within; it is an integral part of the body's security system. Pain,

---

2. The use of the terms *speech* and *word* should not be understood in the colloquial physical sense, but in the metaphysical, phenomenological sense. When I say the slave is speechless, I mean to convey the idea that he is deprived of the meaningfulness of speech.
3. Exodus 12:26-27; 13:8, 14-15; Deuteronomy 6:20-25.

Rabbi Joseph B. Soloveitchik

as instinctual reaction, is immediate and non-reflective. As such, it is not restricted to humans: the beast is also exposed to and acquainted with pain.

Suffering or distress, in contradistinction to pain, is not a sensation but an experience, a spiritual reality known only to humans (the animal does not suffer). This spiritual reality is encountered by man whenever he stands to lose either his sense of existential security (as in the case of an incurable disease) or his existential dignity (as in the case of public humiliation). Whenever a merciless reality clashes with the human existential awareness, man *suffers* and finds himself in distress.

5

The animal is exposed to pain; so is the slave. When the slave meets with pain he reacts like the animal, uttering a sharp, shrill sound. However, the howl of the beast, like the shriek of the slave, lasts a moment in the darkness and hush of the night. In a split second all is silent again. There is no aftermath to the pain-sensation of the animal or the slave; there follows no complaint, no request, no protest, no question of why and what. The slave does not know suffering, lacking, as he does, the very existential need-awareness which generates suffering. He is never in distress because he has no *human* needs. The needs of a slave are, like his shriek, not human: the etiology of his needs is exclusively biological. The absence of suffering mitigates the sharpness of pain. Former inmates of concentration camps have told me that they had, with the passage of time, become inured to any pain or torture, as if they had been totally anesthetized. They were dumb beings. They not only stopped speaking, but ceased to emit coherent sounds, as well.

Redemption, Prayer, Talmud Torah

6

The Zohar tells us:

תא חזי: כתיב "הן בני ישראל לא שמעו אלי ואיך ישמעני פרעה
ואני ערל שפתים". מאי "ואני ערל שפתים"? והא בקדמיתא כתיב
"לא איש דברים אנכי וגו' כי כבד פה וכבד לשון אנכי" וקב"ה
הוה אותיב ליה "מי שם פה לאדם" וגו' והוא אמר "ואנכי אהיה
עם פיך". ס"ד דלא הוה כן והשתא אמר "ואני ערל שפתים"? אי
הכי אן הוא מלה דאבטח ליה קב"ה בקדמיתא? אלא רזא איהו,
משה קלא ודבור דאיהו מלה דיליה הוה בגלותא והוה איהו אטים
לפרשא מלין, ובגין דא אמר "ואיך ישמעני פרעה" בעוד דמילה
דילי איהי בגלותא דיליה דהא לית לי מלה דהא אנא קלא מלה גרע
דאיהי בגלותא. ועל דא שתף קב"ה לאהרן בהדיה. תא חזי כל זמנא
דדבור הוה בגלותא קלא אסתלק מניה ומלה הוה אטים קול, כד
אתא משה אתא קול ומשה הוה קול בלא מלה בגין דהוה בגלותא
וכל זמנא דדבור הוה בגלותא משה אזיל קלא בלא דבור. והכי אזיל
עד דקריבו לטורא דסיני ואתיהיבת אורייתא ובההוא זמנא אתחבר
קלא בדבור וכדין מלה מליל, הדא הוא דכתיב ה"ד "וידבר אלקים
את כל הדברים האלה". וכדין משה אשתכח שלים במילה כדקא
יאות קול ודבור כחדא בשלימו, ועל דא משה אתרעים דמלה גרע
מניה בר ההוא זמנא דמלילת לאתרעמא עלוי בזמנא דכתיב "ומאז
באתי אל פרעה לדבר בשמך" מיד "וידבר אלקים אל משה".

And Moses spake before the Lord, saying: "Behold, the children of Israel have not harkened unto me; how then shall Pharaoh hear me, who am of uncircumcised lips?" How did Moses dare say this? Had not the Holy One already promised him, when he said that he was not eloquent, that He "will be with his mouth" (Exodus 4:10-12)? Or did the Holy One not keep His promise? However, there is here an inner meaning. Moses was then in the grade of "Voice," and the grade of "Utterance" was then in exile. Hence he said, "How shall Pharaoh hear me, seeing that my 'utterance' is in bondage to him, I being only 'voice, and lacking 'utterance.'" Therefore God joined with him Aaron, who was "utterance" without "voice." When Moses came, the Voice appeared, but it was "a voice without speech." This lasted until Israel approached Mount Sinai to receive the Torah. Then the Voice was united with the Utterance, and the word was spoken, as it says, "and the Lord *spake* all these words" (Exodus 20:1). Then Moses was in full possession of the Word, Voice and Word being united. That was the cause of Moses' complaint (v. 23), that he lacked the word save at the time when it broke forth in complaint and "God spake to Moses."[4]

The text divides the process of redemption in three stages. First it identifies bondage with the absence of both word and meaningful sound, with total silence. Then redemption begins with finding sound while the word is still absent. Finally, with the finding of both sound and word, redemption attains it full realization.

Before Moses came there was not even a single sound. No complaint was lodged, no sigh, no cry uttered. Only an agonizing un-human shriek would penetrate the weird silence of the night. The slaves were gloomy, voiceless and mute. The women did not cry when their infants were snatched from their arms; the men kept quiet when they were mercilessly tortured by the slave drivers. Torture was taken for granted. They thought this was the way it had to be. The pain did not precipitate suffering. They were unaware of any need.

---

4. Zohar, *Vaera*, 11:22.

Redemption, Prayer, Talmud Torah

When Moses came, the sound, or the voice, came into being: כי אתא משה אתא קול. Moses, by defending the helpless Jew, restored sensitivity to the dull slaves. Suddenly they realized that all that pain, anguish, humiliation and cruelty, all the greed and intolerance of man vis-à-vis his fellow man is evil. This realization brought in its wake not only sharp pain but a sense of suffering as well. With suffering came loud protest, the cry, the unuttered question, the wordless demand for justice and retribution. In short, the dead silence of non-existence was gone; the voice of human existence was now heard.

ויהי בימים הרבים ההם וימת מלך מצרים ויאנחו בני ישראל מן העבדה ויזעקו ותעל שועתם אל האלקים מן העבדה.

And it came to pass in the course of the many days that the king of Egypt died and the children of Israel sighed by reason of the bondage and they cried and their cry came up unto God...[5]

Why hadn't they cried before Moses acted? Why were they silent during the many years of slavery that preceded Moses' appearance? They had lacked the need-awareness, and experienced no need, whether for freedom, for dignity, or for painless existence. They did not rebel against reality; they lacked the tension that engenders suffering and distress. The voice was restored to them at the very instant they discovered, emotionally, their need awareness and became sensitive to pain in a human fashion. Moses' protest precipitated this change.

---

5. Exodus 2:23.

Rabbi Joseph B. Soloveitchik

7

Even Moses, the Zohar emphasizes, who helped the people move from the silent periphery to the great center, did not acquire the word until he and the people reached Mount Sinai. Although Moses had the existential *awareness* of need, he had not as yet discovered the *logos* of need which would, in turn, have endowed him with the charisma of speech. When the Almighty advised him that he had been chosen to be the redeemer of the people, Moses argued and was reluctant to accept the mission because the word was not, as yet, given to him; therefore, he was *aral sefatayim* (slow of speech).[6] Surely Moses had protested; he had killed the tyrant, rebuked the wicked Jew, etc. What he lacked was the logical understanding of the teleology of the *galut* experience, as well as the firm faith in the destiny of the slave-community. He did not believe that those slaves would ever be liberated. Hence, while Moses, and with him the whole community, had already broken out of their silence, they had yet to find the word. Only at Sinai was the *logos*, both as word and as knowledge, revealed to him. He finally understood the covenantal past, beheld the vision of a great future whose realization was dependent upon him.

II

I

This story is indicative, not only of the political slave of antiquity, but of slavery today, as well. Slavery is not only a juridic-economic institution of the past; it is also a way of life which is still a reality. The unfree man differs, existentially, from the free man: one may, existentially, be a slave in the midst of political and economic freedoms. To use Biblical terminology, slavery constitutes a *tohu va-vohu* existence.

---

6. Ibid. 6:12.

Redemption, Prayer, Talmud Torah

What does the existential slave look like? How does existential *tohu va-vohu* express itself in daily life? There are two basic characteristics of which we may avail ourselves in identifying the slavish *tohu va-vohu* existence in every era: 1) anonymity; 2) ignorance.

How does the anonymity of man express itself? In the tragic reality of being forgotten. The history of mankind is the history of countless millions of forgotten, nameless people, who have vanished into nothingness, along with their grave marks (if any). Men come and go, like Peretz's Bontsche Schweig,[7] without leaving a trace or making a mark. The anonymity which envelops man is part of the curse God imposed upon Adam. Man experiences his anonymity as a great loneliness.

If this is true of man in the past, it is certainly true of modern man. Urban life has contributed greatly to the anonymity and loneliness-experience of the individual. When Kohelet said: כי בהבל בא ובחשך ילך ובחשך שמו יכסה, "For he comes in vanity and departs in darkness and his name is covered in darkness,"[8] he referred not only to the unknown timid soul, to the poor and meek, but to everybody: the great ruler, the daring warrior, the captain of industry and the famous orator. All of these people live in anonymity and darkness and are existentially peripheral, mute beings. All of us, no matter how popular, are people whose destiny consists in being forgotten.

---

7. This is how Bontche Schweig is described: "Bontche Schweig's death made no impression whatsoever. No one knew who Bontche was. Bontche lived mutely and died quietly. Like a silent shadow did he pass through our world. At Bontche's circumcision no toasts were raised, no glasses were clinked. At his Bar Mitzvah no rousing speech was delivered. He lived in anonymity like a grey minute grain of sand on the beach of a stormy sea, among millions of identical sand particles ... no one noticed that one of the particles was picked up by the storm and carried across the sea."
8. Ecclesiastes 6:4.

2

Man is not only anonymous, but ignorant as well. Let me qualify: when I say that man is ignorant, I do not refer to his scientific achievements; in this area modern man is clever and ingenious. What man fails to comprehend is not the world around him, but the world within him, particularly his destiny, and the needs of which he is supposed to have a clear awareness.

Many would say that to accuse modern man of being unaware of his needs is absurd. The reverse, they would maintain, is true. Modern man is aware of many needs; in fact, there are too many needs which claim his attention. An entire technology is bent upon generating more and more needs in order to give man the opportunity to derive pleasure through the gratification of artificially-fabricated needs.

Though this assertion is true, it does not contradict my previous statement that contemporary man is unaware of his needs. Man is surely aware of many needs, but the needs he is aware of are not always his own. At the very root of this failure to recognize one's truly worthwhile needs lies man's ability to misunderstand and misidentify himself, i.e., to lose himself. Quite often man loses himself by identifying himself with the wrong image. Because of this misidentification, man adopts the wrong table of needs which he feels he must gratify. Man responds quickly to the pressure of certain needs, not knowing *whose* needs he is out to gratify. At this juncture, sin is born. What is the cause of sin, if not the diabolical habit of man to be mistaken about his own self? Let me add that man fails to recognize himself because he is man. As man, he was cursed by the Almighty, condemned to misuse his freedom and to lose his own self. In other words, adoption of a wrong table of needs is a part of the human tragic destiny.

Redemption, Prayer, Talmud Torah

The confusion about one's true needs is typical of man as man, without distinction of life-experience. Does the young man understand his basic needs? If he did, we would have no problem of crime, drugs and permissiveness in general. Is the middle-aged man oriented toward his real needs; does he know what is relevant and what is irrelevant to him? If he did, there would be fewer deaths from heart disease. Does the old man know what should and what should not matter to him? Let me speak for myself: I know that I am perplexed that my fears are irrational, incoherent. At times I am given over to panic; I am afraid of death. At other times I am horrified by the thought of becoming, God forbid, incapacitated during my lifetime. One of my greatest fears is related to the observance of the Day of Atonement: I am fearful that I might be compelled, because of weakness or sickness, to desecrate this holiest of all days.

I don't know what to fear, what not to fear; I am utterly confused and ignorant. Modern man is, indeed, existentially a slave, because he is ignorant and fails to identify his own needs.

3

This principle, that a man often perceives as his own the needs of some other self, finds expression in several areas of Halacha. The central position which *teshuva* occupies in our system of thought is based upon our belief that man is free to establish himself or to determine his own identity, in either a positive or a negative manner. While, in sin, man mis-identifies and alienates himself from himself, in the case of *teshuva* he reverses the process of mis-identification: he discovers himself, and "returns" to his true self.

Two Halachic legal concepts, *hatarat nedarim* (the absolution of vows and oaths) and *asmakhta* (collateral security with condition of forfeiture beyond the amount secured), rest upon the doctrine of man as self-fooling being. In the case of *asmakhta* the law declares certain agreements null and void, if they were engendered in a mood of overconfidence on the part of one of the participants. We accept that opinion in Halacha which maintains that a contract precipitated by such optimistic anticipation is not always valid,[9] although the contract was signed voluntarily, without coercion. The individual who made the promise is regarded as hiving been guided by the wrong table of needs, pressed upon him by the "phony I." Consequently, the agreement is invalid: it was signed, in effect, by the wrong person.

The same principle underlies the concept of *hatarat nedarim*. What is *hatarat nedarim*? One takes a vow or an oath, to engage in or refrain from an action. Later he discovers the difficulties connected with the execution or his vow or oath. He appears before three people, and they dissolve the vow or the oath, by subjecting him to a cross-examination which results in the conclusion that, had he anticipated the hardship engendered by compliance with the vow or oath, he would never have committed himself. The question arises: why is he absolved? The taking of the vow or oath was a free act; nobody constrained him to do so. The answer is the same as for *asmakhta*. In substituting the pseudo-I, with its wrong table of needs, for the true self and the right table of needs, the individual has ceased to be the author of his own deed, of his vow or oath.

III

I

How can one redeem oneself from this kind of slavery? The redemption from Egypt was completely an act of the Almighty:

---

9. *Baba Batra* 168a.

Redemption, Prayer, Talmud Torah

liberty and speech were returned to the people by Him in an act of endless grace and benevolence: ועברתי בארץ מצרים ... אני ולא מלאך, "And I shall pass in the land of Egypt ... I and not an angel."[10] The case of existential slavery is, however, different: it is up to man, who is charged with the task of redeeming himself from a shadow existence. God wills man to be creator – his first job is to create himself as a complete being. Man, the mute being, must search for speech and find it, all by himself. Man comes into our world as a hylic, amorphous being. He is created in the image of God, but this image is a challenge to be met, not a gratuitous gift. It is up to man to objectify himself, to impress form upon a latent formless personality and to move from the hylic, silent periphery toward the center of objective reality. The highest norm in our moral code is: *to be*, in a total sense, to liberate oneself from the bondage of a shadowy *mé on* (to use Platonic jargon) and to move toward the wide spaces of *ontos on*, real, true being, full of song and joy, the crystal-clear accents of speech. Man was commanded to redeem himself in order to attain full being. This can be achieved only through prayer: ונצעק אל ה׳, "And we cried unto God."[11] The redemption from Egypt was initiated through prayer.

2

Judaism, in contradistinction to mystical quietism, which recommended toleration of pain, wants man to cry out aloud against any kind of pain, to react indignantly to all kinds of injustice or unfairness. For Judaism held that the individual who displays indifference to pain and suffering, who meekly reconciles himself to the ugly, disproportionate and unjust in life,

---

10. Exodus 12:12, as interpreted in *Mekhilta* and *Haggadah*.
11. Deuteronomy 26:7.

Rabbi Joseph B. Soloveitchik

is not capable of appreciating beauty and goodness. Whoever permits his legitimate needs to go unsatisfied will never be sympathetic to the crying needs of others. A human morality based on love and friendship, on sharing in the travail of others, cannot be practiced if the person's own need-awareness is dull, and he does not know what suffering is. Hence Judaism rejected models of existence which deny human need, such as the angelic or the monastic. For Judaism, need-awareness constitutes part of the definition of human existence. Need-awareness turns into a passional experience, into a suffering awareness.[12] *Dolorem ferre ergo sum* – I suffer, therefore I am – to paraphrase Descartes' *cogito ergo sum*. While the Cartesian cogito would also apply to an angel or even to the devil, our inference is limited to man: neither angel nor devil knows suffering.

Therefore, prayer in Judaism, unlike the prayer of classical mysticism, is bound up with the human needs, wants, drives and urges, which make man suffer. Prayer is the doctrine of human needs. Prayer tells the individual, as well as the community, what his, or its, genuine needs are, what he should, or should not, petition God about. Of the nineteen benedictions in our *Amida*, thirteen are concerned with basic human needs, individual as well as social-national.[13] Even two of the last three benedictions (*Retzeh* and *Sim Shalom*) are of a petitional nature. The person in need is summoned to pray. Prayer and *tzara* (trouble) are inseparably linked. Who prays? Only the sufferer prays.[14] If man does not find himself in narrow straits, if he is not troubled by anything, if he knows not what *tzara* is, then he need not pray. To a happy man, to contented man, the secret of

---

12. The role of *yissurin* (suffering) is discussed by Nahmanides in *Shaar HaGemul*.
13. Vide Maimonides, *Hil. Tefillah* 1:4.
14. Vide Nahmanides, comments on Maimonides' *Sefer HaMitzvot*, Positive Commandment 5.

Redemption, Prayer, Talmud Torah

prayer was not revealed. God needs neither thanks nor hymns. He wants to hear the outcry of man, confronted with a ruthless reality. He expects prayer to rise from a suffering world cognizant of its genuine needs. In short, through prayer man finds himself. Prayer enlightens man about his needs. It tells man the story of his hidden hopes and expectations. It teaches him how to behold the vision and how to strive in order to realize this vision, when to be satisfied with what one possesses, when to reach out for more. In a word, man finds his need-awareness, himself, in prayer. Of course, the very instant he finds himself, he becomes a redeemed being.

3

What is the structure of liberation through prayer? We find, upon analysis, that the process of redemption of the individual and the community through prayer is similar to the redemption from Egypt, as described by the Zohar. There are three stages: 1) no prayer at all – the silence of atrophy, the absence of a need-awareness; 2) an outcry, a voice, saturated with suffering and sadness; 3) the birth of the word, i.e., the birth of prayer through the word.

It is in the second stage, with the awakening of the need-awareness, that prayer makes its entry. This level of intermediate prayer is not yet *tefilla* but *tze'aka*, a human outcry: *Shome'a kol tze'aka* – "Hearer of outcry" – is a Divine attribute. There is, as yet, no word, no sentence; although the emotional awareness has awakened, the *logos* of need is still dormant, silent. There is not yet a clear understanding of what one is crying for. There is distress and loud human weeping. *Tze'aka* is primordial prayer, the voice restored, the word still lacking.

In the final stage, the word appears; the outcry is transformed into speech. Man, at this level, not only feels his needs but understands them as well; there is a logic of prayer which opens up to man when he is in possession of the word.

4

At this stage prayer is not just a shriek or a cry anymore. It is rather a well-defined thought, a clear conception. *Tze'aka* turns into *tefilla*. We do not know the exact semantics of the term *tefilla*. Yet one thing is clear: the term is related to thinking, judging, discrimination.[15] In short, prayer is connected with the intellectual gesture. The hierarchy of needs, clearly defined and evaluated, is to be found in the text of the *Amida*, where not only the emotional need-awareness, but also the *logos* of need and with it the human being himself are redeemed. The outpouring of the heart merges with the insights of the mind. To pray means to discriminate, to evaluate, to understand, in other words, to ask intelligently. I pray for the gratification of some needs since I consider them worthy of being gratified. I refrain from petitioning God for the satisfaction of other wants because it will not enhance my dignity.

5

Tze'aka is not only a phenomenological idea, but a Halachic-religious reality. *Tefilla*, though it represents a more advanced awareness, does not replace *tze'aka*, but co-exists with it. Man, even the most sophisticated and educated, frequently resembles the baby who cries because of pain, but does not know how to alleviate the pain.

In Halachic liturgy, prayer at the stage of *tze'aka* is called *Selichot*. There are four distinctive characteristics of *Selichot*:

---

15. E.g. Exodus 21:22; 1 Samuel 2:25.

1. recital of the thirteen attributes of mercy (י״ג מידות);[16]
2. confession (*viddui*);
3. repetition of short sentences distinguished by simplicity of form (e.g. מי שענה לאברהם... הוא יעננו, "May He who answered Abraham ... answer us");
4. reading of prophetic verses of petition or praise.

The main distinction between *tefilla* (represented by the *Amida*) and *tze'aka* (as represented by *Selichot*) consists in the absence of strict formulation in the case of *Selichot*. Prayer as *tze'aka* lacks the gradual development of theme, the structural formalism, and the etiquette-like orderliness which Halacha required of the *mitpallel*, the prayerful person.[17]

While *tefilla* is a meditative-reflective act, *tze'aka* is immediate and compulsive. The *tzo'ek* is not bound by any requirements as to language, flow of words, sequences of premises and conclusions. He is free to submit his petition, no matter how informal, so long as he feels pain, and knows that only God can free him from the pain.

IV

I

When prayer rises from *tze'aka* to *tefilla*, an experience in which the whole human personality is involved, it merges with another redemptive experience, namely, that of *talmud Torah*, Torah study. It was for a good reason that Moses and Ezra integrated *keri'at haTorah*, Torah reading, into the framework of *tefilla*.[18]

---

16. Vide *Rosh haShanah* 17b.
17. These structures are elaborated in Maimonides, *Hil. Tefillah*, chs. 4–5.
18. *Baba Kama* 82a.

Rabbi Joseph B. Soloveitchik

Without *talmud Torah*, it would be difficult for *tefilla* to assure man of total redemption.

2

What does Torah do for the redemption of man? Permit me to quote the following Talmudic passage:

דרש ר' שמלאי: למה הולד דומה במעי אמו? ... נר דלוק לו על ראשו וצופה ומביט מסוף העולם ועד סופו, שנאמר "בהלו נרו עלי ראשי לאורו אלך חשך"....

ומלמדין אותו כל התורה כולה, שנאמר "ויורני ויאמר לי יתמך דברי לבך שמר מצותי וחיה", ואומר "בסוד אלו-ה עלי אהלי"....
וכיון שבא לאויר העולם בא מלאך וסטרו על פיו ומשכחו כל התורה כולה, שנאמר "לפתח חטאת רובץ".

> R. Simlai delivered the following discourse: What does an embryo resemble when it is in the bowels of its mother? ... A light burns above its head and it looks and sees from one end of the world to the other, as it is said, "When his lamp shined above my head, and by His light I walked through darkness" (Job 23:3)....
>
> It is also taught all the Torah from beginning to end, for it said, "And he taught me, and said unto me: 'Let thy heart hold fast my words, keep my commandments and live'" (Proverbs 4:4), and it is also said, "When the converse of God was upon my tent" (Job 29:4).... As soon as it sees the light an angel approaches, slaps it on its mouth and causes it to forget all the Torah completely, as it said, "Sin coucheth at the door" (Genesis 4:7).[19]

---

19. *Niddah* 30b.

Redemption, Prayer, Talmud Torah

There is an obvious question: If the angel makes the baby forget everything he taught it, why did he bother to teach the embryo at all? The answer is again obvious. R. Simlai wanted to tell us that when a Jew studies Torah he is confronted with something which is not foreign and extraneous, but rather intimate and already familiar, because he has already studied it, and the knowledge was stored up in the recesses of his memory and became part of him. He studies, in effect, his own stuff. Learning is the recollection of something familiar.[20] The Jew studying Torah is like the amnesia victim who tries to reconstruct from fragments the beautiful world he once experienced. In other words, by learning Torah man returns to his own self; man finds himself, and advances toward a charted, illuminated and speaking I-existence. Once he finds himself, he finds redemption.

3

Intellectual redemption through the study of Torah resembles, in its structure, the redemption through prayer which, in turn, is modeled upon the Zohar's description of the redemption from Egypt. We may speak of it in terms of the Zohar's three stages: 1) We are silent – there is complete intellectual insensitivity and total unconcern. 2) Voice is restored, but speech is lacking; sounds, not words, are audible – cognitive curiosity and amazement awaken. We begin to be annoyed because we do not understand. We are perturbed by something which is a part of ourselves but which we are unable to define. 3) The word breaks through; there is clear and distinct cognition. Our intellect begins to speak. We have found the charismatic endowment,

---

20. One is reminded, by sheer terminological association, of the Platonic doctrine of anamnesis.

namely Torah, in the depths of our personality, and, *ipso facto*, we have found ourselves.

Once man gains insight into his true self, by activating the intellect, he finds himself on the road towards discovering ultimate redemption. When man recognizes himself, he dissipates not only ignorance, but also the mist of anonymity. He is not unknown anymore: he knows himself, and finds freedom in his knowledge. He is aware of his needs because he prays; he is aware of his intellectual creative capacities because he studies. He is sure that the needs are his own, and that the intellectual capacities are a part of himself. This twofold knowledge is cathartic and redemptive.

V

1

When *tefilla* and *talmud Torah* unite in one redemptive experience, prayer becomes *avoda shebalev*.[21] What does this term denote? Not the service by the heart, but the *offering* of the heart; Judaic dialectic plays "mischievously" with two opposites, two irreconcilable aspects of prayer. It announces prayer as self-acquisition, self-discovery, self-objectification and self-redemption. By sensitizing and logicizing the awareness of need, man delivers himself from the silence and from non-being and becomes an I, a complete being who belongs to himself. At this level, prayer makes man feel whole: at this level, prayer means self-acquisition. Yet there is another aspect to prayer: prayer is an act of giving away. Prayer means sacrifice, unrestricted offering of the whole self, the returning to God of body and soul, everything one possesses and cherishes. There is an altar

---

21. *Sifre* (Deuteronomy 11:13) interprets ולעבדו both with regards to *tefilla* and *talmud Torah* (cited by Maimonides, *Sefer haMitzvot*, Positive Commandment 5).

Redemption, Prayer, Talmud Torah

in heaven upon which the archangel Michael offers the souls of the righteous. Thrice daily we petition God to accept our prayers, as well as the fires – the self-sacrifices of Israel – on that altar (ואשי ישראל ותפילתם באהבה תקבל ברצון).[22] Prayer is rooted in the idea that man belongs, not to himself, but that God claims man, and that His claim to man is not partial but total. God the Almighty sometimes wills man to place himself, like Isaac of old, on the altar, to light the fire and to be consumed as a burnt offering. Does not the story of the *akeda* tell us about the great, awesome drama of man giving himself away to God? Of course Judaism is vehemently opposed to human sacrifice. The Bible speaks with indignation and disdain of child sacrifice; physical human sacrifice was declared abominable.[23] Yet the idea that man belongs to God, without qualification, and that God, from time to time, makes a demand upon man to return what is God's to God is an important principle in Judaism. God claimed Moses' life: He demanded the return of body and soul without permitting him to cross the Jordan. Moses complied, and willingly died the "Death by Kiss." God claimed Isaac and Abraham gave Isaac away. What does prayer mean in the light of all this? The restoration of God's ownership rights, which are absolute, over everything He owns. The call ויאמר קח נא את בנך את יחידך אשר אהבת את יצחק וכו' והעלהו שם לעלה, "Take thy son, thy only son, whom you love so much, … and bring him as a burnt offering"[24] is addressed to all men. In response to this call, man engages in prayer, as sacrificial performance.

---

22. *Tosfot Menahot* 110a ד"ה ומיכאל.
23. E.g. Deuteronomy 12:31.
24. Genesis 22:2.

2

A new equation emerges: prayer equals sacrifice. Initially prayer helps man discover himself, through understanding and affirmation of his need-awareness. Once the task of self-discovery is fulfilled, man is summoned to ascend the altar and return everything he has just acquired to God. Man who was told to create himself, objectify himself, and gain independence and freedom for himself, must return everything he considers his own to God.

Confrontation

The Biblical account of the creation of man portrays him at three progressive levels.

At the first level, he appears as a simple natural being. He is neither cognizant of his unique station in the cosmos nor burdened by the awareness of his paradoxical capability of being concurrently free and obedient, creative to the point of self-transcendence and submissive in a manner bordering on self-effacement. At this stage, natural man is irresponsive to the pressure of both the imperative from without and the "ought" from within – the inner call of his humanity surging *de profundis – mima'amakim*. For the norm either from within or from without addresses itself only to man who is sensitive to his own incongruity and tragic dilemma. The illusory happy-mindedness of natural man stands between him and the norm. Natural man, unaware of the element of tension prevailing between the human being and the environment of which he is an integral part, has no need to live a normative life and to find redemption in surrender to a higher moral will. His existence is unbounded, merging harmoniously with the general order of things and events. He is united with nature, moving straightforwards, with the beast and the fowl of the field, along an unbroken line of mechanical life-activities, never turning around, never glancing backwards, leading an existence which is neither fraught with contradiction nor perplexed by paradoxes, nor marred by fright.

> ... וכל שיח השדה טרם יהיה בארץ ובל עשב השדה טרם יצמח
> ואדם אין לעבד את האדמה. ואד יעלה מן הארץ והשקה את כל
> פני האדמה. וייצר ה' א' את האדם עפר מן האדמה ויפח באפיו
> נשמת חיים ויהי האדם לנפש חיה.

> And every plant of the field was not yet in the earth and every herb of the field had not yet grown ... and there was no man to till the ground. But there went up a mist from the earth and watered the whole face of the ground. And the Lord God formed the man of the dust of the ground and breathed into his nostrils the breath of life and the man became a living soul.[1]

Man who was created out of the dust of the ground, enveloped in a mist rising from the jungle, determined by biological immediacy and mechanical necessity, knows of no responsibility, no opposition, no fear, and no dichotomy, and hence he is free from carrying the load of humanity.

---

1. Genesis 2:5–7. While the Biblical phrase *nefesh chaya* (a living soul) refers to natural man, Onkelos' *ruach memalela* (a speaking spirit) is related to a typologically more advanced stage.

Confrontation

In a word, this man is a non-confronted being. He is neither conscious of his assignment vis-a-vis something which is outside of himself nor is he aware of his existential otherness as a being summoned by his Maker to rise to tragic greatness.

2

When I refer to man at the level of naturalness, I have in mind not the *Urmensch* of bygone times but modern man. I am speaking not in anthropological but typological categories. For non-confronted man is to be found not only in the cave or the jungle but also in the seats of learning and the halls of philosophers and artists. Non-confrontation is not necessarily restricted to a primitive existence but applies to human existence at all times, no matter how cultured and sophisticated. The *hêdoné*-oriented, egocentric person, the beauty-worshipper, committed to the goods of sense and craving exclusively for boundless aesthetic experience, the voluptuary, inventing needs in order to give himself the opportunity of continual gratification, the sybarite, constantly discovering new areas where pleasure is pursued and happiness found and lost, leads a non-confronted existence. At this stage, the intellectual gesture is not the ultimate goal but a means to another end – the attainment of unlimited aesthetic experience. Hence, non-confronted man is prevented from finding himself and bounding his existence as distinct and singular. He fails to realize his great capacity for winning freedom from an unalterable natural order and offering this very freedom as the great sacrifice to God, who wills man to be free in order that he may commit himself unreservedly and forfeit his freedom.

Beauty, uncouth and unrefined but irresistible, seducing man and contributing to his downfall, emerges in the Biblical arena for the first time – according to the Midrash quoted by

Rabbi Joseph B. Soloveitchik

Nahmanides (Genesis 4:22) – in the person of Naamah (the name signifies pleasantness), the sister of Tubal-Cain.

ומדרש אחר לרבותינו שהיא האשה היפה היא מאד שממנה טעו בני אלהים והיא הנרמזת בפסוק "ויראו בני האלהים את בנות האדם."

> Our sages offered another Midrashic interpretation, that Naamah was the fairest of all women, who seduced the sons of the mighty, and it is she who is referred to in the verse: "and the sons of the mighty saw the daughters of man that they were fair."

Her seductive charms captivated the sons of the mighty and led to their appalling disregard for the central divine norm enjoining man from reaching out for the fascinating and beautiful that does not belong to him. The sons of the mighty yielded to the hedonic urge and were unable to discipline their actions. They were a non-confronted, non-normative group. They worshipped beauty and succumbed to its overwhelming impact.

Naamah, the incarnation of unhallowed and unsublimated beauty, is, for the Midrash, not so much an individual as an idea, not only a real person but a symbol of unredeemed beauty. As such, she appears in the Biblical drama in many disguises. At times her name is Delilah, seducing Samson; at other times she is called Tamar, corrupting a prince. She is cast in the role of a princess or queen, inflicting untold harm upon a holy nation and kingdom of priests whose king, the wisest of all men, abandoned his wisdom when he encountered overpowering beauty. The Book of Wisdom (Proverbs) portrays her as the anonymous woman with an "impudent face" who "lieth in wait at every corner" and the Aggadah – also cited here by

Nahmanides – as the beautiful queen of the demons, tempting man and making him restless.

No less than their seductress, the sons of the mighty also represent a universal type. Non-confronted man – whether he be a primitive caveman, the king depicted in Ecclesiastes, or a modern counterpart – is dominated by two characteristics: he can deny himself nothing, and he is aware of neither the indomitable opposition he is bound to meet in the form of a restrictive outside, nor of the absurdity implied in man's faith that the beautiful is a source of pleasure rather than one of frustration and disillusionment. The aesthete of today, like the aesthete of old, is prisoner of – no matter what her name – beauty unethicized and unreclaimed from aboriginal immediacy. He enjoys a sense of oneness with the natural scheme of events and occurrences and his transient successful performance encourages him to strive for the absurd – an unopposed and uncontradicted hedonic *modus existentiae*.

ויטע ה' אלקים גן בעדן מקדם וישם שם את האדם אשר יצר.
ויצמח ה' אלקים מן האדמה כל עץ נחמד למראה וטוב למאכל
ועץ החיים בתוך הגן ועץ הדעת טוב ורע.

And the Lord God planted a garden eastward in Eden and there He put the man whom He had formed. And out of the ground the Lord God caused to grow every tree that is desirable to the sight and good for food; the tree of life in the midst of the garden and the tree of knowledge of good and evil.[2]

---

2. Genesis 2:8–9. Maimonides translated *tov vara* into aesthetic terms as "pleasing and displeasing." Paradisical man, violating the divine commandment by eating from the tree of knowledge, suspended the ethical and replaced it with the aesthetic experience (*Guide of the Perplexed* I, 2).

Rabbi Joseph B. Soloveitchik

Man depicted in these verses is hedonically-minded and pleasure-seeking, having at his disposal a multitude of possibilities of sense-gratification. Before him stretches a vast garden with an almost endless variety of trees desirable and good, tempting, fascinating, and exciting the boundless fantasy with their glamorous colors.

3

At the second level, natural man, moving straightforward, comes suddenly to a stop, turns around, and casts, as an outsider, a contemplative gaze upon his environment. Even the most abandoned voluptuary becomes disillusioned like the king of Ecclesiastes and finds himself encountering something wholly other than his own self, an outside that defies and challenges him. At this very moment, the separation of man from cosmic immediacy, from the uniformity and simplicity which he had shared with nature, takes place. He discovers an awesome and mysterious domain of things and events which is independent of and disobedient to him, an objective order limiting the exercise of his power and offering opposition to him. In the wake of this discovery, he discovers himself. Once self-discovery is accomplished, and a new I-awareness of an existence which is limited and opposed by a non-I outside emerges, something new is born – namely, the divine norm. ויצו ה׳ אלקים על האדם – "And the Lord God commanded the man."[3] With the birth of the norm, man becomes aware of his singularly human existence which expresses itself in the dichotomous experience of being unfree, restricted, imperfect and unredeemed, and, at the same time, being potentially powerful, great and exalted,

---
3. Genesis 2:4.

uniquely endowed, capable of rising far above his environment in response to the divine moral challenge. Man attains his unique identity when, after having been enlightened by God that he is not only a committed but also a free person, endowed with power to implement his commitment, he grasps the incommensurability of what he is and what he is destined to be, of the *vayehi* and *yehi*.

God, in answer to Moses' inquiry, gave His name as *Ehyeh asher Ehyeh* – I am what I am. God is free from the contradiction between potentiality and actuality, ideal and reality. He is pure actuality, existence par excellence.[4] Man, however, is unable to state of himself *ehyeh asher ehyeh* since his real existence always falls short of the ideal which his Maker set up for him as the great objective. This tragic schism reflects, in a paradoxical fashion, human distinctiveness and grandeur.

Simultaneously with man's realization of his inner incongruity and complete alienation from his environment, the human tragic destiny begins to unfold. Man, in his encounter with an objective world and in his assumption of the role of a subject who asks questions about something hitherto simple, forfeits his sense of serenity and peace. He is no longer happy, he begins to examine his station in this world and he finds himself suddenly assailed by perplexity and fear, and especially loneliness. ויאמר ה' אלקים לא טוב היות האדם לבדו, "And the Lord God said: 'It is not good that the man should be alone.'"[5] The I-experience is a passional one, and real man is born amid the pains of confrontation with an "angry" environment of which he had previously been an integral part.

---

4. See *Guide of the Perplexed* I, 63.
5. Genesis 2:18.

Rabbi Joseph B. Soloveitchik

Confronted man is called upon to choose either of two alternatives:

1. To play an active role as a subject-knower, utilizing his great endowment, the intellect, and trying to gain supremacy over the objective order. However, this performance is fraught with difficulty because knowledge is gained only through conflict, and the intellectual performance is an act of conquest.[6] The order of things and events, in spite of its intrinsic knowability and rationality, does not always respond to human inquiry and quite often rejects all pleas for a cooperative relationship. The subject-knower must contest a knowable object, subdue it and make it yield its cognitive contents.[7]
2. Man may despair, succumb to the overpowering pressure of the objective outside and end in mute resignation, failing

---

6. The Latin *objectus*, derived from *objicere*, to oppose, the German *Gegenstand*, denoting something standing opposite, the Hebrew *hefetz*, having the connotation of something intensely desired but not always attainable, are quite indicative of the element of tension which is interwoven into the logical subject-knower knowable-object relationship.
7. The element of tension in the subject-object relationship is a result not of sin but of the incongruity of "attitudes" on the part of the confronters, The attitude of man is one of dominion, while the "attitude" on the part of the objective order is one of irresponsiveness. The knowable object refuses to surrender to the subject-knower. The result of man's sin was not the emergence of tension and resistance – since this state of affairs prevailed even before man's expulsion from Paradise – but the change from tension to frustration, from a creative, successful performance to defeat. In imposing this metaphysical curse upon man, God decreed that the latter, in spite of all his glorious achievements, be finally defeated by death and ignorance. Judaism does not believe that man will ever succeed in his bold attempt to unravel the *mysterium magnum* of being and to control nature as a whole. The human cognitive and technological gestures, Judaism maintains, have a chance to succeed only in small sectors of reality. קוץ ודרדר תצמיח לך, "Thorns and thistles shall it bring forth to thee" (Genesis 3:18).

Confrontation

to discharge his duty as an intellectual being, and thus dissolving an intelligent existence into an absurd nightmare.

Of course, the Torah commanded man to choose the first alternative, to exercise his authority as an intelligent being whose task consists in engaging the objective order in a cognitive contest. We have always rejected the nirvana of inaction because the flight from confrontation is an admission of the bankruptcy of man. When man became alienated from nature and found himself alone, confronted by everything outside of him, God brought the "animal of the field and every fowl of the heaven unto the man to see what he would call it ... and the man gave name to all the beasts and the fowl of the heaven and to every animal of the field." ויצר ה׳ אלקים מן האדמה כל חית השדה ואת כל עוף השמים ויבא אל האדם לראות מה יקרא לו... ויקרא האדם שמות לכל הבהמה ולעוף השמים ולכל חית השדה.⁸ Man no longer marched straightforward with the brutes of the field and the forest. He made an about-face and confronted them as an intelligent being remote from and eager to examine and classify them. God encouraged him to engage in the most miraculous of all human gestures – the cognitive. Confronted Adam responded gladly because he already realized that he was no longer a part of nature but an outsider, a singular being, endowed with intelligence. In his new role, he became aware of his loneliness and isolation from the entire creation. ולאדם לא מצא עזר כנגדו, "And for the man [God] had not found a helpmeet opposite him."⁹ As a lonely being, Adam discovered his great capacity for facing and dominating the non-human order.¹⁰

---

8. Genesis 2:19–20.
9. Genesis 2:20.
10. See Nahmanides, Genesis 2:9.

Rabbi Joseph B. Soloveitchik

4

The Book of Genesis, after describing the four rivers which flow from the Garden of Eden, offers us a new account of the placing of Adam in this garden.

ויקח ה' אלקים את האדם וינחהו בגן עדן לעבדה ולשמרה.

And the Lord God took the man and placed him in the Garden of Eden to cultivate it and to keep it.

This sentence in Genesis 2:15 is almost a verbatim repetition of Genesis 2:8, yet the accounts differ in two respects.

First, in the second account, the Bible uses a verb denoting action preceding the placing of man in the Garden of Eden – "And the Lord God *took* (*vayikah*) the man and placed him" – whereas in the previous account, the verb "he placed," *vayasem*, is not accompanied by any preliminary action on the part of the Almighty. The expression *vayikah* does not occur in the first account. Second, there is no mention in the previous account of any assignment given to man, while this account does specify that man was charged with the task of cultivating and keeping the garden.

The reason for these variations lies in the fact that the two accounts are related to two different men. The first story, as we have previously indicated, is of non-confronted man carried by the mighty tide of a uniform, simple, non-reflective life, who was placed in the Garden of Eden for one purpose only – to pursue pleasure, to enjoy the fruit of the trees without toil, to live in ignorance of his human destiny, to encounter no problem and to be concerned with no obligation. As we stated previously, non-confronted man is a non-normative being. The second story is of confronted man who began to appraise

Confrontation

critically his position vis-a-vis his environment and found his existential experience too complex to be equated with the simplicity and non-directedness of the natural life-stream. This man, as a subject-knower facing an almost impenetrable objective order, was dislocated by God from his position of naturalness and harmonious being and placed in a new existential realm, that of confronted existence. Confronted man is a displaced person. Having been taken out of a state of complacency and optimistic naiveté, he finds the intimate relationship between him and the order of facticity ending in tension and conflict. The verb *vayikah* signifies that God removed man from one dimension and thrust him into another – that of confronted existence. At this phase, man, estranged from nature, fully aware of his grand and tragic destiny, became the recipient of the first norm – ויצו ה׳ אלקים על האדם, "And the Lord God commanded the man." The divine imperative burst forth out of infinity and overpowered finite man.

Alas, not always does creative man respond readily to the divine normative summons which forms the very core of his new existential status as a confronted being. All too often, the motivating force in creative man is not the divine mandate entrusted to him and which must be implemented in full at both levels, the cognitive and the normative, but a demonic urge for power. By fulfilling an incomplete task, modern creative man falls back to a non-confronted, natural existence to which normative pressure is alien. The reason for the failure of confronted man to play his role fully lies in the fact that, while the cognitive gesture gives man mastery and a sense of success, the normative gesture requires of man surrender. At this juncture, man of today commits the error which his ancestor, Adam of old, committed by lending an attentive ear to the demonic whisper, "Ye shall be as God, knowing good and evil."

5

There is, however, a third level which man, if he is longing for self-fulfillment, must ascend. At this level, man finds himself confronted again. Only this time it is not the confrontation of a subject who gazes, with a sense of superiority, at the object beneath him, but of two equal subjects, both lonely in their otherness and uniqueness, both opposed and rejected by an objective order, both craving for companionship. This confrontation is reciprocal, not unilateral. This time the two confronters stand alongside each other, each admitting the existence of the other. An aloof existence is transformed into a together-existence.

ויאמר ה׳ אלקים לא טוב היות האדם לבדו אעשה לו עזר כנגדו...
ויבן ה׳ אלקים את הצלע אשר לקח מן האדם לאשה ויבאה אל האדם.

And the Lord God said, It is not good that the man should be alone. I will make a helpmeet opposite him ... And the Lord God made the rib which he had taken from the man into a woman and brought her unto man.[11]

God created Eve, another human being. Two individuals, lonely and helpless in their solitude, meet, and the first community is formed.

The community can only be born, however, through an act of communication. After gazing at each other in silence and defiance, the two individuals involved in a unique encounter begin to communicate with each other. Out of the mist of muteness the miraculous word rises and shines forth. Adam suddenly begins to talk – ויאמר האדם, "And the man said." He addresses

---

11. Genesis 2:18, 22.

himself to Eve, and with his opening remark, two fenced-in and isolated human existences open up, and they both ecstatically break through to each other.

The word is a paradoxical instrument of communication and contains an inner contradiction. On the one hand, the word is the medium of expressing agreement and concurrence, of reaching mutual understanding, organizing cooperative effort, and uniting action. On the other hand, the word is also the means of manifesting distinctness, emphasizing incongruity, and underlining separateness. The word brings out not only what is common in two existences but the singularity and uniqueness of each existence as well. It emphasizes not only common problems, aspirations and concerns, but also uniquely individual questions, cares and anxieties which assail each person. Our sages, in explaining the graphic difference between the open and closed *mem*, spoke of *ma'amar satum* and *ma'amar patu'ah* – the enigmatic and the clear or distinct phrase. They felt that the word at times enlightens, at times, confounds; at times, elucidates, and at other times, emphasizes the unintelligible and unknowable.

When Adam addressed himself to Eve, employing the word as the means of communication, he certainly told her not only what united them but also what separated them. Eve was both enlightened and perplexed, assured and troubled by his word. For, in all personal unions such as marriage, friendship, or comradeship, however strong the bonds uniting two individuals, the *modi existentiae* remain totally unique and hence, incongruous, at both levels, the ontological and the experiential. The hope of finding a personal existential equation of two human beings is rooted in the dangerous and false notion that human existences are abstract magnitudes subject to simple mathematical processes. This error lies at the root of the philosophies of the corporate state and of mechanistic behaviorism. In fact, the closer two individuals get to know each other, the more aware they become of the metaphysical distance separating them. Each one exists in a singular manner, completely absorbed in his individual awareness which is egocentric and exclusive. The sun of existence rises with the birth of one's self-awareness and sets with its termination. It is beyond the experiential power of an individual to visualize an existence preceding or following his.

It is paradoxical yet nonetheless true that each human being lives both in an existential community, surrounded by friends, and in a state of existential loneliness and tension, confronted by strangers. In each to whom I relate as a human being, I find a friend, for we have many things in common, as well as a stranger, for each of us is unique and wholly other. This otherness stands in the way of complete mutual understanding. The gap of uniqueness is too wide to be bridged. Indeed, it is not a gap, it is an abyss. Of course, there prevails, quite often, a harmony of interests – economic, political, social – upon which two individuals focus their attention. However, two people glancing at the same object may continue to lead isolated, closed-in existences. Coordination of interests does not spell an existential union. We frequently engage in common enterprise and we prudently pursue common goals, travelling temporarily along parallel roads, yet our destinations are not the same. We are, in the words of the Torah, an *ezer* – a helpmeet to each other, yet at the same time, we experience the state of *kenegdo* – we remain different and opposed to each other.[12] We think, feel and respond

---

12. The interpretation of *kenegdo* as "opposing" was accepted by our Talmudic sages. See *Yebamot* 63a.

Confrontation

to events not in unison but singly, each one in his individual fashion. Man is a social being, yearning for a together-existence in which services are exchanged and experiences shared, and a lonely creature, shy and reticent, fearful of the intruding cynical glance of his next-door neighbor. In spite of our sociability and outer-directed nature, we remain strangers to each other. Our feelings of sympathy and love for our confronter are rooted in the surface personality and they do not reach into the inner recesses of our depth personality, which never leaves its ontological seclusion and never becomes involved in a communal existence.

In a word, the greatness of man manifests itself in his dialectical approach to his confronter, in ambivalent acting toward his fellowman, in giving friendship and hurling defiance, in relating himself to, and at the same time, retreating from him. In the dichotomy of *ezer* and *kenegdo* we find our triumph as well as our defeat.

Modern man, who did not meet to the fullest the challenge of confrontation on the second level, does not perform well at the level of personal confrontation either. He has forgotten how to master the difficult dialectical art of *ezer kenegdo* – of being one with and, at the same time, different from, his human confronter, of living in community and simultaneously in solitude. He has developed the habit of confronting his fellow man in a fashion similar to that which prevails at the level of subject-object relationship, seeking to dominate and subordinate him instead of communicating and communing with him. The wondrous personal confrontation of Adam and Eve is thus turned into an ugly attempt at depersonalization. Adam of today wants to appear as master-hero and to subject Eve to his rule and dominion, be it ideological, religious, economic, or political. As a matter of fact, the divine curse addressed to Eve after she sinned, וְהוּא יִמְשָׁל בָּךְ, "and he shall rule over thee,"[13] has found its fulfillment in our modern society. The warm personal relationship between two individuals has been supplanted by a formal subject-object relationship which manifests itself in a quest for power and supremacy.

II

I

We Jews have been burdened with a twofold task; we have to cope with the problem of a double confrontation. We think of ourselves as human beings, sharing the destiny of Adam in his general encounter with nature, and as members of a covenantal community which has preserved its identity under most unfavorable conditions, confronted by another faith community. We believe we are the bearers of a double charismatic load, that of the dignity of man, and that of the sanctity of the covenantal community. In this difficult role, we are summoned by God, who revealed Himself at both the level of universal creation and that of the private covenant, to undertake a double mission – the universal human and the exclusive covenantal confrontation.

Like his forefather, Jacob – whose bitter nocturnal struggle with a mysterious antagonist is so dramatically portrayed in the Bible – the Jew of old was a doubly confronted being. The emancipated modern Jew, however, has been trying, for a long time, to do away with this twofold responsibility which weighs heavily upon him. The Westernized Jew maintains that it is impossible to engage in both confrontations, the universal and the covenantal, which, in his opinion, are mutually exclusive. It is, he argues, absurd to stand shoulder to shoulder with mankind preoccupied with the cognitive-technological gesture

---

13. Genesis 3:16.

for the welfare of all, implementing the mandate granted to us by the Creator, and to make an about-face the next instant in order to confront our comrades as a distinct and separate community. Hence, the Western Jew concludes, we have to choose between these two encounters. We are either confronted human beings or confronted Jews. A double confrontation contains an inner contradiction.

What is characteristic of these single-confrontation philosophers is their optimistic and carefree disposition. Like natural Adam of old, who saw himself as part of his environment and was never assailed by a feeling of being existentially different, they see themselves as secure and fully integrated within general society. They do not raise any questions about the reasonableness and justification of such an optimistic attitude, nor do they try to discover in the deep recesses of their personality commitments which transcend mundane obligations to society.

The proponents of the single-confrontation philosophy (with the exception of some fringe groups) do not preach complete de-Judaization and unqualified assimilation. They also speak of Jewish identity (at least in a religious sense), of Jewish selfhood and the natural will for preservation of the Jewish community as a separate identity. As a matter of fact, quite often they speak with great zeal and warmth about the past and future role of Judaism in the advancement of mankind and its institutions. However, they completely fail to grasp the real nature and the full implications of a meaningful Jewish identity.

2

This failure rests upon two misconceptions of the nature of the faith community. First, the single-confrontation philosophy continues to speak of Jewish identity without realizing that this term can only be understood under the aspect of singularity and otherness.

Rabbi Joseph B. Soloveitchik

There is no identity without uniqueness. As there cannot be an equation between two individuals unless they are converted into abstractions, it is likewise absurd to speak of the commensurability of two faith communities which are individual entities.

The individuality of a faith community expresses itself in a threefold way. First, the divine imperatives and commandments to which a faith community is unreservedly committed must not be equated with the ritual and ethos of another community. Each faith community is engaged in a singular normative gesture reflecting the numinous nature of the act of faith itself, and it is futile to try to find common denominators. Particularly when we speak of the Jewish faith community, whose very essence is expressed in the Halachic performance which is a most individuating factor, any attempt to equate our identity with another is sheer absurdity. Second, the axiological awareness of each faith community is an exclusive one, for it believes – and this belief is indispensable to the survival of the community – that its system of dogmas, doctrines and values is best fitted for the attainment of the ultimate good. Third, each faith community is unyielding in its eschatological expectations. It perceives the events at the end of time with exultant certainty, and expects man, by surrender of selfish pettiness and by consecration to the great destiny of life, to embrace the faith that this community has been preaching throughout the millennia. Standardization of practices, equalization of dogmatic certitudes, and the waiving of eschatological claims spell the end of the vibrant and great faith experience of any religious community. It is as unique and enigmatic as the individual himself.

The second misconception of the single-confrontation philosophy consists in not realizing the compatibility of the two roles. If the relationship of the non-Jewish to the Jewish world had conformed to the divine arrangement for one human being to

Confrontation

meet the other on the basis of equality, friendship and sympathy, the Jew would have been able to become fully involved together with the rest of humanity in the cosmic confrontation. His covenantal uniqueness and his additional mandate to face another faith community as a member of a different community of the committed would not have interfered in the least with his readiness to and capability of joining the cultural enterprise of the rest of humanity. There is no contradiction between coordinating our cultural activity with all men and at the same time confronting them as members of another faith community. As a matter of fact even within the non-Jewish society, each individual sees himself under a double aspect: first, as a member of a cultural-creative community in which all are committed to a common goal and, at the same time, as an individual living in seclusion and loneliness.

Unfortunately, however, non-Jewish society has confronted us throughout the ages in a mood of defiance, as if we were part of the subhuman objective order separated by an abyss from the human, as if we had no capacity for thinking logically, loving passionately, yearning deeply, aspiring and hoping. Of course, as long as we were exposed to such a soulless, impersonal confrontation on the part of non-Jewish society, it was impossible for us to participate to the fullest extent in the great universal creative confrontation between man and the cosmic order. The limited role we played until modern times in the great cosmic confrontation was not of our choosing. Heaven knows that we never encouraged the cruel relationship which the world displayed toward us. We have always considered ourselves an inseparable part of humanity and we were ever ready to accept the divine challenge, מלאו את הארץ וכבשה, "Fill the earth and subdue it,"[14] and the responsibility implicit in human existence.

---

14. Genesis 1:28.

Rabbi Joseph B. Soloveitchik

We have never proclaimed the philosophy of *contemptus* or *odium seculi*. We have steadily maintained that involvement in the creative scheme of things is mandatory.

Involvement with the rest of mankind in the cosmic confrontation does not, we must repeat, rule out the second personal confrontation of two faith communities, each aware of both what it shares with the other and what is singularly its own. In the same manner as Adam and Eve confronted and attempted to subdue a malicious scoffing nature and yet nevertheless encountered each other as two separate individuals cognizant of their incommensurability and uniqueness, so also two faith communities which coordinate their efforts when confronted by the cosmic order may face each other in the full knowledge of their distinctness and individuality.

We reject the theory of a single confrontation and instead insist upon the indispensability of the double confrontation. First, as we have mentioned previously, we, created in the image of God, are charged with responsibility for the great confrontation of man and the cosmos. We stand with civilized society shoulder to shoulder over against an order which defies us all. Second, as a charismatic faith community, we have to meet the challenge of confronting the general non-Jewish faith community. We are called upon to tell this community not only the story it already knows – that we are human beings, committed to the general welfare and progress of mankind, that we are interested in combatting disease, in alleviating human suffering, in protecting man's rights, in helping the needy, *et cetera* – but also what is still unknown to it, namely, our otherness as a metaphysical covenantal community.

3

It is self-evident that a confrontation of two faith communities is possible only if it is accompanied by a clear assurance that

Confrontation

both parties will enjoy equal rights and full religious freedom. We shall resent any attempt on the part of the community of the many to engage us in a peculiar encounter in which our confronter will command us to take a position beneath him while placing himself not alongside of but above us. A democratic confrontation certainly does not demand that we submit to an attitude of self-righteousness taken by the community of the many which, while debating whether or not to "absolve" the community of the few of some mythical guilt, completely ignores its own historical responsibility for the suffering and martyrdom so frequently recorded in the annals of the history of the few, the weak, and the persecuted.

We are not ready for a meeting with another faith community in which we shall become an object of observation, judgment and evaluation, even though the community of the many may then condescendingly display a sense of compassion with the community of the few and advise the many not to harm or persecute the few. Such an encounter would convert the personal Adam-Eve meeting into a hostile confrontation between a subject-knower and a knowable object. We do not intend to play the part of the object encountered by dominating man. Soliciting commiseration is incongruous with the character of a democratic confrontation. There should rather be insistence upon one's inalienable rights as a human being, created by God.

In light of this analysis, it would be reasonable to state that in any confrontation we must insist upon four basic conditions in order to safeguard our individuality and freedom of action.

First, we must state, in unequivocal terms, the following. We are a totally independent faith community. We do not revolve as a satellite in any orbit. Nor are we related to any other faith community as "brethren" even though "separated." People confuse two concepts when they speak of a common

Rabbi Joseph B. Soloveitchik

tradition uniting two faith communities such as the Christian and the Judaic. This term may have relevance if one looks upon a faith community under an historico-cultural aspect and interprets its relationship to another faith community in sociological, human, categories describing the unfolding of the creative consciousness of man. Let us not forget that religious awareness manifests itself not only in a singular apocalyptic faith experience but in a mundane cultural experience as well. Religion is both a divine imperative which was foisted upon man from without and a new dimension of personal being which man discovers within himself. In a word, there is a cultural aspect to the faith experience which is, from a psychological viewpoint, the most integrating, inspiring and uplifting spiritual force. Religious values, doctrines and concepts may be and have been translated into cultural categories enjoyed and cherished even by secular man. All the references throughout the ages to universal religion, philosophical religion, *et cetera*, are related to the cultural aspect of the faith experience of which not only the community of believers but a pragmatic, utilitarian society avails itself as well. The cultural religious experience gives meaning and directedness to human existence and relates it to great ultimates, thus enhancing human dignity and worth even at a mundane level.

Viewing the relationship between Judaism and Christianity under this aspect, it is quite legitimate to speak of a cultural Judeo-Christian tradition for two reasons. First, Judaism as a culture has influenced, indeed, molded the ethicophilosophical Christian world-formula. The basic categories and premises of the latter were evolved in the cultural Judaic orbit. Second, our Western civilization has absorbed both Judaic and Christian elements. As a matter of fact, our Western heritage was shaped by a combination of three factors, the

Confrontation

classical, Judaic, and Christian, and we could readily speak of a Judeo-Hellenistic-Christian tradition within the framework of our Western civilization. However, when we shift the focus from the dimension of culture to that of faith – where total unconditional commitment and involvement are necessary – the whole idea of a tradition of faiths and the continuum of revealed doctrines which are by their very nature incommensurate and related to different frames of reference is utterly absurd, unless one is ready to acquiesce in the Christian theological claim that Christianity has superseded Judaism.

As a faith individuality, the community of the few is endowed with intrinsic worth which must be viewed against its own meta-historical backdrop without relating to the framework of another faith community. For the mere appraisal of the worth of one community in terms of the service it has rendered to another community, no matter how great and important this service was, constitutes an infringement of the sovereignty and dignity of even the smallest of faith communities. When God created man and endowed him with individual dignity, He decreed that the ontological legitimacy and relevance of the individual human being is to be discovered not without but within the individual. He was created because God approved of him as an autonomous human being and not as an auxiliary being in the service of someone else. The ontological purposiveness of his existence is immanent in him. The same is true of a religious community, whose worth is not to be measured by external standards.

Therefore, any intimation, overt or covert, on the part of the community of the many that it is expected of the community of the few that it shed its uniqueness and cease existing because it has fulfilled its mission by paving the way for the community of the many, must be rejected as undemocratic and contravening the very idea of religious freedom. The small community has as much right to profess its faith in the ultimate certitude concerning the doctrinal worth of its world formula and to behold its own eschatological vision as does the community of the many. I do not deny the right of the community of the many to address itself to the community of the few in its own eschatological terms. However, building a practical program upon this right is hardly consonant with religious democracy and liberalism.

Second, the *logos*, the word, in which the multifarious religious experience is expressed does not lend itself to standardization or universalization. The word of faith reflects the intimate, the private, the paradoxically inexpressible cravings of the individual for and his linking up with his Maker. It reflects the numinous character and the strangeness of the act of faith of a particular community which is totally incomprehensible to the man of a different faith community. Hence, it is important that the religious or theological *logos* should not be employed as the medium of communication between two faith communities whose modes of expression are as unique as their apocalyptic experiences. The confrontation should occur not at a theological, but at a mundane human level. There, all of us speak the universal language of modern man. As a matter of fact, our common interests lie not in the realm of faith, but in that of the secular orders.[15] There, we all face a powerful antagonist, we all have to contend with a considerable number of matters of great concern. The relationship between two communities must be outer-directed and related to the secular

---

15. The term "secular orders" is used here in accordance with its popular semantics. For the man of faith, this term is a misnomer. God claims the whole, not a part of man, and whatever He established as an order within the scheme of creation is sacred.

orders with which men of faith come face to face. In the secular sphere, we may discuss positions to be taken, ideas to be evolved, and plans to be formulated. In these matters, religious communities may together recommend action to be developed and may seize the initiative to be implemented later by general society. However, our joint engagement in this kind of enterprise must not dull our sense of identity as a faith community. We must always remember that our singular commitment to God and our hope and indomitable will for survival are non-negotiable and non-rationalizable and are not subject to debate and argumentation. The great encounter between God and man is a wholly personal private affair incomprehensible to the outsider – even to a brother of the same faith community. The divine message is incommunicable since it defies all standardized media of information and all objective categories. If the powerful community of the many feels like remedying an embarrassing human situation or redressing an historic wrong, it should do so at the human ethical level. However, if the debate should revolve around matters of faith, then one of the confronters will be impelled to avail himself of the language of his opponent. This in itself would mean surrender of individuality and distinctiveness.

Third, we members of the community of the few should always act with tact and understanding and refrain from suggesting to the community of the many, which is both proud and prudent, changes in its ritual or emendations of its texts. If the genuinely liberal dignitaries of the faith community of the many deem some changes advisable, they will act in accordance with their convictions without any prompting on our part. It is not within our purview to advise or solicit. For it would be both impertinent and unwise for an outsider to intrude upon the most private sector of the human existential experience, namely, the way in which a faith community expresses its relationship to God. Non-interference with and non-involvement in something which is totally alien to us is a *conditio sine qua non* for the furtherance of good-will and mutual respect.

Fourth, we certainly have not been authorized by our history, sanctified by the martyrdom of millions, to even hint to another faith community that we are mentally ready to revise historical attitudes, to trade favors pertaining to fundamental matters of faith, and to reconcile "some" differences. Such a suggestion would be nothing but a betrayal of our great tradition and heritage and would, furthermore, produce no practical benefits. Let us not forget that the community of the many will not be satisfied with half measures and compromises which are only indicative of a feeling of insecurity and inner emptiness. We cannot command the respect of our confronters by displaying a servile attitude. Only a candid, frank and unequivocal policy reflecting unconditional commitment to our God, a sense of dignity, pride and inner joy in being what we are, believing with great passion in the ultimate truthfulness of our views, praying fervently for and expecting confidently the fulfillment of our eschatological vision when our faith will rise from particularity to universality, will impress the peers of the other faith community among whom we have both adversaries and friends. I hope and pray that our friends in the community of the many will sustain their liberal convictions and humanitarian ideals by articulating their position on the right of the community of the few to live, create, and worship God in its own way, in freedom and with dignity.

4

Our representatives who meet with the spokesmen of the community of the many should be given instructions similar to those enunciated by our patriarch Jacob when he sent his agents to meet his brother Esau.

> ויצו את הראשון לאמר כי יפגשך עשו אחי ושאלך לאמר למי אתה ואנה תלך ולמי אלה לפניך ואמרת לעבדך ליעקב מנחה היא שלוחה לאדני לעשו והנה גם הוא אחרינו. ויצו גם את השני גם את השלישי גם את כל ההלכים אחרי העדרים לאמר כדבר הזה תדברון אל עשו במצאכם אתו.

> And he commanded the foremost, saying, When Esau my brother meeteth thee and asketh thee, saying: Whose art thou and whither goest thou? And whose are these before thee? Then thou shalt say, They are thy servant Jacob's; it is a present sent unto my lord Esau, and behold he also is behind us. And he commanded also the second, and the third and all that followed the droves, saying, In this manner shall ye speak unto Esau when ye find him.[16]

What was the nature of these instructions? Our approach to and relationship with the outside world has always been of an ambivalent character, intrinsically antithetic, bordering at times on the paradoxical. We relate ourselves to and at the same time withdraw from, we come close to and simultaneously retreat from the world of Esau. When the process of coming nearer and nearer is almost consummated, we immediately begin to retreat quickly into seclusion. We cooperate with the members of other faith communities in all fields of constructive human endeavor, but, simultaneously with our integration into the general social framework, we engage in a movement of recoil and retrace our steps. In a word, we belong to the human society and, at the

---

16. Genesis 32:18–20.

same time, we feel as strangers and outsiders. We are rooted in the here and now reality as inhabitants of our globe, and yet we experience a sense of homelessness and loneliness as if we belonged somewhere else. We are both realists and dreamers, prudent and practical on the one hand, and visionaries and idealists on the other. We are indeed involved in the cultural endeavor and yet we are committed to another dimension of experience. Our first patriarch, Abraham, already introduced himself in the following words: גר ותושב אנכי עמכם, "I am a stranger and sojourner with you."[17] Is it possible to be both – *ger vetoshav* – at the same time? Is not this definition absurd since it contravenes the central principle of classical logic that no cognitive judgment may contain two mutually exclusive terms? And yet, the Jew of old defied this time-honored principle and did think of himself in contradictory terms. He knew well in what areas he could extend his full cooperation to his neighbors and act as a *toshav*, a resident, a sojourner, and at what point this gesture of cooperation and goodwill should terminate, and he must disengage as if he were a *ger*, a stranger. He knew in what enterprise to participate to the best of his ability and what offers and suggestions, however attractive and tempting, to reject resolutely. He was aware of the issues on which he could compromise, of the nature of the goods he could surrender, and vice versa, of the principles which were not negotiable and the spiritual goods which had to be defended at no matter what cost. The boundary line between a finite idea and a principle nurtured by infinity, transient possessions and eternal treasures, was clear and precise. Jacob, in his instructions to his agents, laid down the rule:

---

17. Genesis 23:4.

Confrontation

כי יפגשך עשו אחי ושאלך לאמר למי אתה ואנה תלך ולמי אלה לפניך?

When Esau my brother meeteth thee and asketh thee, saying: Whose art thou, and whither goest thou and whose are these before thee?

My brother Esau, Jacob told his agents, will address to you three questions. "Whose art thou?" To whom do you as a metaphysical being, as a soul, as a spiritual personality belong? "And whither goest thou?" To whom is your historical destiny committed? To whom have you consecrated your future? What is your ultimate goal, your final objective? Who is your God and what is your way of life? These two inquiries are related to your identity as members of a covenantal community. However, Jacob continued, my brother Esau will also ask a third question: "And whose are these before thee?" Are you ready to contribute your talents, capabilities and efforts toward the material and cultural welfare of general society? Are you ready to present me with gifts, oxen, goats, camels and bulls? Are you willing to pay taxes, to develop and industrialize the country? This third inquiry is focused on temporal aspects of life. As regards the third question, Jacob told his agents to answer in the positive. "It is a present sent unto my lord Esau." Yes, we are determined to participate in every civic, scientific, and political enterprise. We feel obligated to enrich society with our creative talents and to be constructive and useful citizens. Yet, pertaining to the first two questions – whose art thou and whither goest thou – Jacob commanded his representatives to reply in the negative, clearly and precisely, boldly and courageously. He commanded them to tell Esau that their soul, their personality, their metaphysical destiny, their spiritual future and sacred commitments, belong exclusively to God and His servant Jacob. "They are thy servant Jacob's," and no human power can succeed in severing the eternal bond between them and God.

This testament handed down to us by Jacob has become very relevant now in the year 1964. We find ourselves confronted again like Jacob of old, and our confronters are ready to address to us the identical three questions: "Whose art thou? Whither goest thou? Whose are these before thee?" A millennia-old history demands from us that we meet the challenge courageously and give the same answers with which Jacob entrusted his messengers several thousand years ago.

STATEMENT ADOPTED BY THE RABBINICAL COUNCIL OF AMERICA AT THE MID-WINTER CONFERENCE, FEBRUARY 3–5, 1964

We are pleased to note that in recent years there has evolved in our country as well as throughout the world a desire to seek better understanding and a mutual respect among the world's major faiths. The current threat of secularism and materialism and the modern atheistic negation of religion and religious values makes even more imperative a harmonious relationship among the faiths. This relationship, however, can only be of value if it will not be in conflict with the uniqueness of each religious community, since each religious community is an individual entity which cannot be merged or equated with a community which is committed to a different faith. Each religious community is endowed with intrinsic dignity and metaphysical worth. Its historical experience, its present dynamics, its hopes and aspirations for the future can only be interpreted in terms of full spiritual independence of and freedom from any relatedness to another faith community. Any suggestion that the historical and meta-historical worth of a faith community be viewed against the backdrop of another faith, and the mere hint that a revision of basic historic attitudes is anticipated, are incongruous with the fundamentals of religious liberty and freedom of conscience and can only breed discord and suspicion. Such an approach is unacceptable to any self-respecting faith community that is proud of its past, vibrant and active in the present and determined to live on in the future and to continue serving God in its own individual way. Only full appreciation on the part of all of the singular role, inherent worth and basic prerogatives of each religious community will help promote the spirit of cooperation among faiths.

It is the prayerful hope of the Rabbinical Council of America that all inter-religious discussion and activity will be confined to these dimensions and will be guided by the prophet Micah (4:5), "Let all the people walk, each one in the name of his god, and we shall walk in the name of our Lord, our God, forever and ever."

ADDENDUM TO THE ORIGINAL
EDITION OF "CONFRONTATION"

The following addendum was written by Rabbi Soloveitchik and published along with "Confrontation" in *A Treasury of Tradition*, New York: Hebrew Publishing Company, 1967, pp. 78–80.

On Interfaith Relationships

The Jewish religious tradition expresses itself in a fusion of universalism and singularism. On the one hand, Jews are vitally concerned with the problems affecting the common destiny of man. We consider ourselves members of the universal community charged with the responsibility of promoting progress in all fields, economic, social, scientific, and ethical. As such, we are opposed to a philosophy of isolationism or esoterism which would see the Jews living in a culturally closed society.

On the other hand, we are a distinctive faith community with a unique commitment, singular relationship to God and a specific way of life. We must never confuse our role as the bearers of a particular commitment and destiny with our role as members of the family of man.

In the areas of universal concern, we welcome an exchange of ideas and impressions. Communication among the various communities will greatly contribute towards mutual understanding and will enhance and deepen our knowledge of those universal aspects of man which are relevant to all of us.

In the area of faith, religious law, doctrine, and ritual, Jews have throughout the ages been a community guided exclusively by distinctive concerns, ideals, and commitments. Our love of and dedication to God are personal and bespeak an intimate relationship which must not be debated with others whose relationship to God has been molded by different historical events and in different terms. *Discussion will in no way enhance or hallow these emotions.*

We are, therefore, opposed to any public debate, dialogue or symposium concerning the doctrinal, dogmatic or ritual aspects of our faith vis-à-vis "similar" aspects of another faith community. We believe in and are committed to our Maker in a specific manner and we will not question, defend, offer apologies, analyze or rationalize our faith in dialogues centered about these "private" topics which express our personal relationship to the God of Israel. We assume that members of other faith communities will feel similarly about their individual religious commitment.

We would deem it improper to enter into dialogues on such topics as: Judaic monotheism and the Christian idea of Trinity; the messianic idea in Judaism and Christianity; the Jewish attitude on Jesus; the concept of the covenant in Judaism and Christianity; the Eucharist mass and Jewish prayer service; the Holy Ghost and prophetic inspiration; Isaiah and Christianity; the priest and the rabbi; sacrifice and the

On Interfaith Relationships

Eucharist; the church and the synagogue – their sanctity and metaphysical nature, etc. There cannot be mutual understanding concerning these topics, *for Jew and Christian will employ different categories and move within incommensurate frames of reference and evaluation.*

When, however, we move from the private world of faith to the public world of humanitarian and cultural endeavors, communication among the various faith communities is desirable and even essential. We are ready to enter into dialogue on such topics as war and peace, poverty, freedom, man's moral values, the threat of secularism, technology and human values, civil rights, etc., which revolve about religious spiritual aspects of our civilization. Discussion within these areas will, of course, be within the framework of our religious outlooks and terminology.

Jewish rabbis and Christian clergymen cannot discuss sociocultural and moral problems as sociologists, historians or cultural ethicists in agnostic or secularist categories. As men of God, our thoughts, feelings, perceptions and terminology bear the imprint of a religious world outlook. We define ideas in religious categories and we express our feelings in a peculiar language which quite often is incomprehensible to the secularist. In discussions we apply the religious yardstick and the religious idiom. We evaluate man as the bearer of God's Likeness. We define morality as an act of *Imitatio Dei*, etc. In a word, even our dialogue at a socio-humanitarian level must inevitably be grounded in universal religious categories and values. However, these categories and values, even though religious in nature and biblical in origin, represent the universal and public – not the individual and private – in religion.

To repeat, we are ready to discuss universal religious problems. We will resist any attempt to debate our private individual commitment.

Publication Information

"The Community." *Tradition* 17:2 (Spring 1978): 7–24.
"Majesty and Humility." *Tradition* 17:2 (Spring 1978): 25–37.
"Catharsis." *Tradition* 17:2 (Spring 1978): 38–54.
"Redemption, Prayer, Talmud Torah." *Tradition* 17:2 (Spring 1978): 55–72.
"Confrontation." *Tradition* 6:2 (Spring 1964): 5–29.
"On Interfaith Relationships." *A Treasury of Tradition*, New York: Hebrew Publishing Company, 1967, 78–80.

The fonts used in this book are from the Garamond family

Maggid Books
*The best of contemporary Jewish thought from
Koren Publishers Jerusalem Ltd.*